unkillable Positivity

~ Forward ~

Where to start? First and foremost, I would not be here, and you would not be reading these words if not for my mother. A mother who had every right to be less, but instead was so much more of a parent than she should have been, given her own experiences as a child. For as long as she was here, she guided me as best as she could and even after her passing, left a legacy that I strive to live up to till this very day. She taught me that it was not only okay, but an absolute necessity to be willing to shift priorities and dreams, for that matter, as life's roads began to twist and turn unexpectedly. ~~~~~~~ to my children, who gave and st~~~~~ ~~~~~~ be grateful for, but to continue~~~~ my best friend, who taught me~~~~~~~~~~ ~r nearly as much as having eac~~~~~~~~ that the depth of our river of fr~~~~~~ thickness of blood.

CW01497128

~ The Lights and the Swing ~

One more time. I need to see the lights of Vegas one more time. A phrase that I audibly muttered to myself as gas filled the tank of my Subaru Outback. MY tank hadn't been full in quite some time, years in fact. Las Vegas was my favorite place to vacation. It was something that I had texted my best friend Chris months ago while battling illness after illness. He thought I had more time; he was wrong. Now, here I was divorced, disabled, bankrupt, dying, homeless, immunocompromised, covered in a bleeding rash, COVID positive with two grand in my pocket at a gas station in Fort Worth, Texas. My breathing was getting shallower, and I had nowhere to turn. I knew I couldn't drive straight through to Vegas, but I also knew that I may have mere days left. I had two Monsters in my cupholders, a full tank of gas, my medications and three days of clothes in a duffle bag. A far cry from the man that I used to be, perhaps more accurately, a mere shell of my former self. In a cold, dead sweat I put Vegas in my navigation as I coughed uncontrollably and headed west hoping that I could see those lights one more time. How could all the triumphs and tragedies of my life have led me here?

Green grass chased by a blue sky and a burning sun. These images comprise my earliest memory. What is yours? I was not particularly young, there was no particular reason for it sticking, but it did. Nothing special occurred that day. Perhaps it was the simplicity that made it memorable and the repetitiveness of simplicity that made it special. Recollection constructs a summer day and being pushed on a swing set by my mother. My mother's words sifted through the summer breeze. I remember having no thought of anything but the immediate moments. She must have recognized the gaze that one only possesses in truly carefree moments. She said, "have not a care in the world Stoney, never do, just swing your life away!" This goal doesn't seem too lofty to a child, but one that quickly becomes unattainable as we make our way through this world.

It is amazing how self-involved we become as we are growing up. That we can somehow be insulated from the realities of the world, a world so seemingly small and controllable. In my mind's eye, I can recall much more detail as to how "carefree" our existence really wasn't.   My swing set was next to our single-wide mobile home in Deer Creek, Oklahoma. My secret hideout came as a courtesy of the skirting of our home falling into disrepair. It was neat to me, an escape from a reality that as of that moment never warranted a retreat. Insulated and untouched by the cruelties of the world. My future was as bright and promising as the blue sky that my torn sneakers reached for each time my mother pushed against my back in attempts to keep her child smiling for just a little longer.

~ *The Woman Who Made Me, Me* ~

To say that my mother was a strong woman would be a gross understatement. She was a daughter of an Army Sargent turned barber, who was rumored to be a decent human being before going off to war. He was a scout, and their life expectancy was mere minutes. He stormed the beach at Normandy and waded through the blood of his fellow soldiers. He made it through D Day and traveled through North Africa, Belgium, France and Sicily. He was shot 3 times, getting hit in the hand, neck, chin and somehow managed to live. Unfortunately, a purple heart was not the only thing that he brought home with him, he brought the war home with him as well. As far as his family was concerned, the purple heart was the only heart that he possessed after the war. My mother endured horrors, some told and others untold, in her childhood that few can imagine. My grandfather showed her 3 things. How to survive, how to cut hair and how to be evil. She did not enjoy the insulation of a carefree existence that she so carefully wrapped me in for as long as she could.

Her reality was different. Her reality was harsh. She honed her survival skills, she was a damn good barber, but she passed on evil. She had a reason to look for a means of escape, a gap in the skirting of a trailer would not do. She wanted to build her clientele as a barber, to follow in his footsteps in a way. She was talented and there was no arguing that. She expressed her ambitions to her father, he replied "you will be what your sister is, or you will be nothing!" My mother's beauty and intelligence were only rivaled by her stubbornness, quick wit and insecurity. She chose nothing for nearly 20 years. My mother's method of escape would have to come in a different form. That escape would come though.

Her escape plan came to fruition in the form of my father. He was her Clark Kent, a Superman with no kryptonite in sight. It was there, however, a fact hidden from my mother's eyes for years and my and my sister's eyes for many more.

~ Lessons from 'Nothing' ~

My childhood memories are flooded with flashes of the imagery and the rambling wisdom of my mother. She chose to be nothing, but by doing so, she was so much more. She was a stay-at-home mom for most of my childhood. She was there, every single day, or so it seems looking back. Every speed bump that came my way, she was there with a metaphorical jackhammer, smoothing out the path that I called life. I was not the only child, but I was the baby. My sister was 6 years my elder and she'd be the first to admit that I was the favorite. She was not mistreated, I was not a frowner, but I was doted on for sure. I wanted for nothing, and I am not even sure how her and my father accomplished that feat.   We were not well off by any stretch of the imagination, but somehow, I never went without.   There was a price to be paid for the attention garnered though, a price for being so much like her.

She was relatively uneducated, again she chose to be 'nothing.' She did not attend college like her sister, but that piece of paper is not the measurement of intelligence, not by a longshot. I remember being about 6 years old sitting in the car outside Pizza Hut when she surprised me with a task. She pulled out a hundred-dollar bill and handed it to me. Now imagine being 6 years old in 1982 and being handed a hundred-dollar bill. My heart pounded with excitement, which quickly morphed into fear. The fear washed over me as I was told that I would go inside by myself and pay for the pizza. She knew how much the pizza was going to cost but would not tell me. She gave me strict instructions to "know" my correct change before the kid at the counter could enter it on the register. I still recall that I was asked for $9.82 and as I handed the bill over, I told the man that my change was $90.18. He looked puzzled but handed me back exactly that. My heart that had been pounding with fear was now beating with pride. Upon my return to the car, my mother approved of the math that I had made quick work of and explained her reasoning. "Trust is fine, but throughout your life people will take advantage of the naïve and you can't afford to be naïve in life." I tried to soak in her cold reasoning on the ride home as the hot cardboard pizza box warmed my legs on that cold winter day. More times than I can count, she force-fed me life lessons at ages that at the time did not seem appropriate for the content, but years later it would all make sense.

~ Numbers...Some for fun. Some Not. ~

She taught me manners, so much so that saying ma'am and sir became a reflex. The act of holding doors open for females was second nature as well. Kindness and manners for the sake of kindness and manners. There was no mention of payoff for these behaviors, not for recognition of any sort, but just because it was the right thing to do and for how it made me feel. She told me that not everyone would thank me for opening a door for them but receiving the thank you was not the point. Again, it was because it was important to her, to us, because in our minds it was the right thing to do.

My mother was a mere 5 foot 3, although her license stated 5 foot 6. My father, not to be outdone was only 5 foot 5, but he had to be taller than her on his license as well. So, he stated his height as 5 foot 7 inches. They were not tall folks, and neither was I. I was not particularly athletic and chose vocal music over sports. I was the first riser kid. The shortest kid in class, even with being held back from starting kindergarten. I was small. I was shy. When I turned 16, I stood five feet flat. Following in my parents' footsteps, I listed my height on my driver's license as 5 foot 2. I felt like I got away with something there.

It was during my teenage years that she began to mention it. It was almost like a joke to her. A joke that she told repeatedly, one that was eventually shortened to a singular word. Fifty. She told me for years that she would be dead by 50. We didn't pay much attention to it, as humans do, we dismiss what we don't want to hear, what we don't want to think about. The table was slowly being set, while no one wanted to partake in the service, it was being set, nonetheless.

~ The Guilt Trip Friendship ~

My teenage years were spent in bowling alleys. It was the first sport in which my lack of stature wasn't a detriment. After all, I was only 5 feet flat when I got my driver's license. I didn't want to bowl originally, in fact my grandfather asked me to bowl in a league, but I told my mother that I thought it was stupid, and I already wasn't the cool kid in school, and this certainly wouldn't help on that front. I will always remember her guilting me into it. Moms are good at that, saying what you don't want to hear to get you to do the things that you don't want to do, yet deep down you know is the right thing to do. "Your grandpa will be dead one day, in the ground forever and you are going feel like an ass if you don't do the only activity that he has EVER asked you to do with him." I lamented and showed up with a forced smile. Much to my surprise, I loved the game. Sure, it was the product of a guilt trip, but it was there that I would end up meeting my best friend, Chris.

Chris was older than I by four months, but so much more advanced in bowling and in mischief. He was a rougher kid, but a black sheep like me. Although for different reasons, a fellow outcast he was indeed. We didn't like each other at first but bonded out of necessity. He worried my mom a bit, I could tell. He was as tough as I was sarcastic. He was already a black belt in martial arts, but the art of friendship had evaded the both of us. My mother pulled me aside and gave me permission to be friends with Chris, but just at the bowling alley to start. I am quite certain she knew that she would not always be around and his roughness in a way made her feel safe. Looking back, I think she saw a bit of herself in him. A rougher childhood and a bit of what I would be like if she hadn't broken the cycle of abuse. Whether he wanted people to know it or not, Chris was a good dude, and she saw it. She knew it, long before he knew it himself. She became a mother figure to Chris. She would never know just how much Chris would save me decades later, but she saw something in him that few did.

~ My Mother's Mistake ~

If you recall, I referred to my father as my mother's Superman. I said, with no kryptonite in sight. It was there however, lurking. I know not the details of his childhood, as that generation didn't talk about the struggles that they faced. They didn't talk about taboo things. I was 10 when I first realized something was wrong. He didn't come home one day, nor the next. He was the sole breadwinner, with that came pressure. The pressure was too great. We moved to Georgia for him to take a different position for work. One that promised less pressure. It didn't deliver on that promise. I remember my mother calling the police frantically and then them showing up. They asked what he might be wearing. She took one look into the closet and rattled off black boots, blue jeans, a black T-shirt, his Army jacket and there's a jar of peanut butter missing. She was spot on as she usually was.

I remember racing up and down the roads of rural Georgia on my go-cart looking for his car but never seeing it. I remember on day three that the phone rang and her begging him to come home and it sounded like he didn't want to come home. I picked up the other phone and heard him crying, I too begged him to come home. It was the first time that I heard my father cry. He made his way home.

I remember riding in the U-Haul with him as we traveled from Georgia to Oklahoma. I asked him what our house would look like. He got quiet for a moment then said, "right now we don't have a home of our own." We would live with my grandparents for a while. Things eventually returned to normal for a bit but would worsen again when I was 16. I remember he went missing again, this time on foot. We searched for him all day. The gun was missing. We gave up for the day and then I saw their closet door move. I pulled it away from the wall and found my father standing behind it like a statue. Unharmed, but unhinged. I told him that we were going to take him to the VA to get him help. I will never forget him saying, "I will never get to come home son." I assured him as best a six-teen year old could and we left for the VA.

We checked him in, and the wait would be long, but he agreed to stay. This shell of a man. It was the first time that he looked small to me. It was late and he agreed not to flee if left to his own devices. My mother and I started for the door. We got to the end of the corridor, and she looked over her shoulder as did I. We could see his bald spot. We could see him waiting for someone to tell him that he was indeed not okay. My mother looked at me and simply said, "I can't leave him here, not like this, not in a place like this. I can take care of him better than they can." To this day, I wonder how differently life would have turned out for more than just myself, if she would have left him there to get the help that he so obviously needed. His mental status would deteriorate for the rest of his days, mom covered as best as she possibly could.

~ *A Little Milk Changes Everything* ~

It was during this time when my mother's choice to be nothing to spite her father came to an end. If you remember, he was a barber. He was also a drunk and his health was failing. One day he climbed behind the wheel of his three on the tree pickup and went to go buy some milk at Braum's. He pulled in and hit the gas instead of the brake and literally drove into the dining area. Luckily no one was seated at the tables where he drove through the plate glass window. He stumbled to the cooler, grabbed a gallon of milk, placed it on the counter with a 5-dollar bill and said, "that'll do it." He stumbled back to his two-toned Chevy, threw it in reverse and backed out of Braum's. He made it home without further incident, but the word was out, and the license plate was jotted down. The police arrived at his home and when he answered the door he slurred, "Is there a problem officer?"

He avoided jail time, paid for damages, gave up his driver's license and a good chunk of his ego. He was cutting hair at $4 a head at his barber shop. My mother stepped in and took over his shop. She got given a chance. My grandfather had all but destroyed his once successful business. A business my mother dreamed of for decades. She now had to rebuild it, 4 dollars at a time. She would become a fixture in the community. She didn't take appointments, she didn't have to, not Judy. Folks would pop their heads into her shop and ask, "how long do you think Judy?" She'd say ungodly things like 2 hours. Their reply? You're worth the wait. Your stories are worth it. You see, she had the gift of gab. I was lucky enough to inherit that gift and even more lucky to be her favorite subject to gab about. She'd close early on Thursdays so she could watch me bowl youth league. On Friday's her customers would ask, what did Stoney shoot yesterday?

~ *Where's the Car?* ~

Every afternoon of league, every tournament in which I competed, mom was there without fail. She had a connection to people and the universe for that matter. She could read situations and people with what seemed like zero effort. She was the only person on the planet that could call me on all my bullshit. She was so in tune with those around her, it bordered on clairvoyant. She could see everything, and a decade ahead of time, she saw her own end.

To say I lived in the bowling alley is an understatement. I went straight there from school and practiced every afternoon until adult leagues started at 6pm every evening. I was going to bowl for a living and nothing would get in my way. As the years progressed, the sport started to decline, but I didn't care. It was the only thing in the world that I loved. It was the place where the world made sense to me. Rough day at school, go throw it hard. Get bullied in the bowling alley, go throw it hard. Life falling apart, go throw it hard. The only person who had more faith in me than myself was my mother. One year the amount of faith she had in me scared the hell out of me!

When my mother grew up, her father's prized possession was his Cadillac. It was a symbol of his arrogance, his ego, and his success as a barber shop owner. My mother had now taken over his shop and built her own following. She purchased a black Lincoln Town Car. It was not expensive, but was long, slick, black and beautiful to her. It was her "Cadillac." It was her other baby, and she did the unthinkable with it because of her faith in me. She sold it without hesitation, without a solid plan of her replacing it.

There was this tournament that paid $100,000 for first place called the High Roller. I was a senior in high school and just old enough to enter it. It happened during my school year so I knew that I would have to wait one more year before I would get to go compete, or so I thought.

I got home from school, but there was no car in the driveway. I walked in to see my mom sitting at the table with a stack of hundred-dollar bills. You see she didn't have the money for the $1100 entry fee, let alone the funds to get us to Vegas and back, but she had faith in me. She sold her car for $3500 and shoved the stack of cash toward me and said, "WE are going to Vegas!" Still not fully understanding what was happening I asked where she came up with the cash. She told me to look in the driveway. I walked to the window and looked. She asked if I could see her car, I said no. She told me she sold it to get me to Vegas. I looked at her like she was crazy, because let's face it, she was. I told her she can't do this; she told me that it was already done. I said let's go get your car back right now, she said too late, I've already mailed your entry, you'll just have to go win enough money in Vegas to replace it! They agreed to hold the car for a few weeks before reselling it. It was up to me to get it back. I had competed in the summer version of this tournament once but was sent home without a dime. I was terrified!

~ *All Kinds of Turbulence* ~

We flew to Vegas together. After all we had no choice, as we didn't have a car. I was quiet on the plane. My main concern was the turbulence and arriving alive in Vegas to let my mother down in one piece. My second concern was whether I would have to pay to fix the armrest that I was surely going to tear off my seat during the horrors of our tumultuous flight to Vegas. So, I did what many of us do. I started talking to God. Well, not so much talking, but instead negotiating. The solemn vow of, "dear God, just get me to the ground safely and I will never get on another flying casket ever again." My anxiety was focused solely on not dying in a fiery crash into the Grand Canyon. That is until we landed safely.   The moment that we landed, I again shifted my anxiety to my impending failure at the tournament. I had never won more than a single match in that bowling center, let alone my new challenge of needing to win 4.

If she doubted me, she never showed it. There was much more to the High Roller than simply being a singular tournament. There were numerous opportunities to make some money. They were called sweepers. All day and most of the night there were chances to make some money back, in other words, chances to win back her car as Johnny Cash would say, one piece at a time. We checked in to the Showboat Hotel/Casino/Bowling Center and unpacked with only about an hour before the first sweeper. The sweeper itself was only two games long. I had never taken part in this type of side action before, which added to the nervousness, but it gave me a chance to loosen up before my first single elimination match in the morning. I laced up and got ready, then our 5 minutes of practice started. Every shot I threw, I learned something, I learned that I had nothing. I had never seen a pattern like this and then before I knew it, practice was over, and the sweeper began. I was dying inside, my mother never shifted in her seat before now, but this time she did just that, she leaned in.

Every pitch I threw, I floundered. If I struck it was luck, and I wasn't lucky often. My entries were prepaid, so I wasn't going further in the hole every shot, but I was running out of opportunities each time I sent the ball down the lane. It was embarrassing and the night wasn't over. I had two sweepers back-to-back, and it seemed that I blinked, and I was practicing on my next pair. I still had nothing. Practice was now over once again. The floundering continued at a blistering pace. It was like Keanu said in The Replacements, quicksand. The harder I fought, the faster and deeper that I sank.

I started much like I had been all night, knowing before I threw it that I wasn't getting there.   I had passed panic and was in desperation mode. I began watching the guys that were striking, they were doing something I had never even thought to attempt. They were standing in front of the ball-return to hook what seemed like the entire lane because they were so dry. I was down to my final frame of game one of the final sweeper, and I was not going to make any money so I sat by mom in defeat. She said only two words, "do it." I looked at her like she was crazy. She had watched her boy for years and today was no exception. She had been watching me, watching the other guys who were getting it done on the lanes.

I walked to the approach and looked over my shoulder to see her leaning forward and she gave me a nod. I walked up in front of the ball return and tried to settle into to my first attempt at lofting the ball over the gutter cap between the lanes. My feet moved forward, and I went for it. What followed was the loudest noise that I had ever heard.

~ Again...Again ~

The noise? It was my ball catching the inside edge of the left-hand gutter and immediately clanging into the gutter. I turned around to see guys laughing and smirking, I wanted to die, then I saw something else. My mother staring at me, nodding and then she mouthed the word "again!" I was in disbelief and defiant. I stood in my regular area again, then heard something, I heard her voice, she said "again" again. It was not in my head, everybody within 4 lanes each way heard it. I was more embarrassed than ever, but I had a decision to make. Defy her and play it safe or take the chance of further humiliation. Well, she was my roommate, and I would never hear the end of it, but there was more to it than that. Who was I to not take the chance? She was the one with skin in the game. She sold her car in faith that I could get it done. I stood back up in front of the ball return and let it rip.

It again was the sound of me catching the lip of the left gutter just as I had before. Yup, I finished the 10th frame with a double gutter in front of some of the best players on the planet. I turned around to more laughs and jabs from guys, but still a determined stare from my mother who mouthed the same damn word, "again."

I of course argued while I waited for my next turn, but to no avail. The final game of the sweeper was starting and I again stood in front of the ball return. I started my feet and let it rip. Again, I caught the lip, I again made the loudest noise imaginable. The laughs continue, but so does the nodding and mouthing of the word "again." I step back in front of the ball return, again I catch the lip. What's the definition of insanity? The laughs are now dying down, replaced with disbelief. Players on each side are now pacing their shots with mine, to avoid being distracted by the noise that still echoes in my mind. Tears welling in my eyes, I start frame 2. I was on the left lane, but still had to loft but I could get a running start if I wanted. I glanced over my shoulder again, my mother nodded and motioned for me to stand in that uncomfortable spot. I walked further up on the approach and gave it a little more. Crack! I caught the lip again. I walk back for my second attempt and hear a player say, "he's a fucking joke!" I looked back praying she hadn't heard it; her look was murderous, and it incensed me. The tears were gone. I stepped back up on the approach, shaking with adrenaline. I started my feet and gave it everything. I cleared the cap and more than that I essentially struck by sparing a full deck of pins. I turned around to a wink from mom with a grin she mouthed "again." I managed to obey 10 more times in a row, finishing the game with 260. I walked out of the center that night winning back $700 of the car fund. My first match was bright and early in the morning.

~ *Missing the Mark* ~

The way the tournament works is this, random draw for lane assignments and therefore randomly draw your opponent. The entry fee was $1100, and it was a single elimination bracket format. My opponent was roughly in his mid-thirties, about twice my age, which in the sport of bowling played to his advantage with experience. The match is just a blur in my memory outside of him staring daggers at me the entire time until the final frame. He finished strong and forced me to fill twenty in the tenth to win by one. This means I could spare then strike, Strike then spare or strike twice, and I would advance to fight another opponent, every shot that game was harder than the one before it. The tenth frame was no exception. I managed to throw it well and struck the first ball in the tenth frame. Now if I struck again, I would proceed to the next match, if I spared, I would progress to the next match as well. I threw the next shot, and I knew immediately that I didn't catch all of it.

I left the 2-10 split. Now here is where math comes into play. If I play it safe and get one, I will tie the guy and force a two frame roll off. If I went for it and spared it, I would win. However, if I cut it a little thin and missed both, I would lose and therefore my hopes of securing the car fund would be down the drain. I didn't like my odds either way but decided to play it safe and just go for one. I signaled to my mom my intention and she agreed. I lined up to hit the 2-pin, my heart sank as the ball left my hand. I immediately knew that I missed.

I did not run the 2-pin down and that would have forced my opponent to a two frame roll off. I missed left badly, although I was the only person in the building that knew I missed that shot. That was the case because I missed just badly enough that when I missed my target left, it resulted in me sparing the split unintentionally. I heard my mom yelling and a few others clapping for what appeared to be a very clutch shot. I advanced, against all odds, I advanced. I walked back to an elated mother who said, "so you decided to go for it!" She beamed with pride, I replied "nope, I missed left" with a straight face. Without missing a beat, she then came back with, "if you hadn't made the right choice to play it safe you would have missed even further left and lost, which means you still won on purpose."   She always had a way of making me feel better no matter what the outcome. Then she hit me with another truth bomb.

~ Boarding 'Pass' ~

She informed me that for me to win enough matches to earn back the car fund, we would then miss our flight home. This little wrinkle plays out as follows, she didn't have enough money for the more expensive flight home over the weekend so booked the cheaper flight that returned before the championship match, before the final couple rounds of the bracket. She figured that if I kept winning, we'd leave with enough money to book another flight. So, I could lose early and get back our flight, which if you remember I made a deal with God never to fly again, or I could keep winning matches, and we would have to figure out transportation which encompassed 1041 miles back home to Oklahoma. I mulled this over before my next match.

I was so caught up in the travel arrangements during my next match that I wasn't even really that nervous. I got up in the tenth needing a mark, a spare or a strike, and I struck my first pitch to end it quickly. The next match was a complex one, but I had 2 sweepers that night that stood between myself and that debacle.

The sweeper went well, and I edged closer to the car fund goal. By the end of the night, I had managed to scrape to just shy of $1300 total. Still a daunting $2200 away from my goal, I was starting to sweat it out, but mom looked as calm as ever. I barely slept that night.

The match that made us miss our flight home once again came down to the tenth frame. I had to mark in the tenth and left a 10 pen on my first attempt. If I spared it we miss our flight, but I make enough to get us back to even on our investment, but must pay for another flight home, which then puts me back in the hole. I go for the spare and hang up a bit in the ball and miss left.

The ball traveled down the lane for what seemed like an eternity. I barely touched the 10 pen and converted the spare. I had now nearly made my mother's investment back but had missed our impending flight out that afternoon by advancing in the bracket. I needed to win yet another match. I would fail to do so.

I listened to my mom on the phone with the airlines for hours, but to no avail. We simply couldn't afford it. Then she got a great and terrible idea for a solution to our travel predicament. She got us a cab to the Las Vegas bus terminal. Do you remember that scene in Planes, Trains and Automobiles where John Candy asks Steve Martin if he'd ever traveled by bus before, then says well your mood probably isn't going to improve much. THAT'S A FACT! I had plenty of time to reflect on the 30-hour bus ride home. I of course was relieved that she would be able to get her car back, but there was more to it than that. That car was more than a car to her. It was a symbol of her success and countless hours spent on her feet cutting hair at $4.00 a head. To her it was showing her father that she could accomplish something on her terms. All those things wrapped up in a $3500 car. It was something so special, yet she put it on the line because she believed in her son, so that perhaps her son would believe in himself when she was no longer on this earth. I then tried to put myself in that position. I simply couldn't imagine that level of selflessness at the tender age of 18, but I was her favorite and maybe that had something to do with it. She and my father continued to support my dream of bowling for a living. I was not in a rush to move out at 18 like most of my peers.

~ My First ~

It was April of 1995, I was bowling in a regional in Enid, Oklahoma at the age of 18. I had just gotten the three required signatures from other professional bowlers so that I could get my pro-card. It was technically my first tournament as a "professional." It was the only thing that I had ever wanted to do, to bowl for a living. The only thing that I had ever really dreamed of up to that point. It was close enough to home that I had quite a few friends that made the trip to show support. I was nervous and knew that I was out of my depth, but I had been taught by my mother that if it is something that you want, you go for it, even if you are terrified. So, I did exactly that, I went for it.

Qualifying was grueling for me. Grueling may be too soft of a descriptor. It was borderline embarrassing. Not that I bowled that terribly, but that I just couldn't really get anything going, especially with a ton of familiar faces trying to cheer me on. I was exhausted by the end of the block, two pitches a frame will do that shit to you. I was an absolute nobody back then and was not required, nor allowed to bowl as a pro in the pro-am. I was happy with that and usually take off quickly after competing, but for some reason, I hung around.   I was walking down the concourse, and I got a sympathetic nod from a touring pro named Billy Young. I walked over and we talked shop for a little while. He was kind and offered words of encouragement, I was grateful for that. Then something caught my eye, or should I say someone...

She was the most beautiful thing that I had ever seen. She was bowling in the Pro-Am as an amateur. Billy caught me staring at her. She was just gorgeous in every conceivable way. She had a smile that just killed me each time I had the privilege of seeing it. Billy was saying words, but they were not registering with me at all. He nudged me on the shoulder to get my attention. He said, "Well, looks like your bowling isn't the only thing on your mind anymore." I grinned in agreement and nodded. I was no longer exhausted. I was in love. Instantly in love.

I stayed and watched her finish her tournament. I had already packed my stuff into my car, so that only thing on my mind was her. Her name was Misty, I started to approach her by her lanes, but I froze and then retreated. She then went to the game room, and I followed her. I had never had a girlfriend, ever. I was so nervous and knew that I was once again out of my depth. I was terrified, but I went for it. She was at the ticket counter and with a very shaky "hi, I'm Stoney." I swung for the fence. You know those scenes in movies where one person is talking, but the other person can hardly hear anything besides their own heart pounding, yeah that was me. I told her that I had to go but asked for her phone number. She then floored me with her response. "On, one condition. You have to promise to take me out on a date." I replied, "I can make that happen." I had a pencil and paper ready. As she read off her number, my hands tremored with excitement. I could barely read it. She saw my hands shake. She was kind enough to not point it out but simply grinned knowing how much I liked her from the moment I met her. We parted ways that night and my 90-minute drive home was an absolute blur. I simply couldn't believe she asked me out on a date, on the spot. I was in heaven!

This was before the days of text messaging. There was no luxury of carefully thought-out replies. It was dialing the phone and hope you don't sound like an idiot. I was not a talker, where the phone is concerned. However, I simply could not hear her voice enough. It was cute, kind, funny and sexy all at once. My favorite thing was that I could literally hear her smile through the phone. I loved it. I loved her!

We spoke a few times that week. I immediately pinned her down for a date on the following Friday night. I offered to pick her up at home, but she opted to have me pick her up at the bowling alley. I changed shirts 4 times before getting in the car. I arrived at the bowling alley a few minutes early, 15 minutes early, and sat in my car searching for the courage to walk in to start our date. My first date. Once again, I had never had a girlfriend before.

~ *Our First Date* ~

I walked through the doors of the bowling alley, knees shaking and heart racing, mind you, that we both worked at the bowling alley, but I had such tunnel vision and lack of interest in the opposite sex, I had never noticed her. Now, however, she had my full attention. I saw Misty standing by the desk. I grabbed her hand and asked if she was ready, and with the most beautiful smile in the world, I knew the answer was yes.

I honestly don't think that I let go of her hand all night. There was just something about her. Something about us. Just the simple act of holding her hand made my soul feel whole for the first time in my life. For the first time, I was all too aware of what I had been missing.

The date itself was such a paradox. I tried so hard, without trying at all. So many things that should have been work, things that should have been orchestrated, those things simply flowed naturally. Her mere presence was intoxicating. Her smile set me on fire and her laugh fed my soul. It was the greatest day of my life up to that point and I didn't want it to end. It had to though, and I went to drop her off. I had never kissed a girl before. I was so nervous but knew that I would hate myself if I didn't summon the courage to kiss her. I was terrified, but I went for it! It was amazing! It was everything that I had hoped it could be. I loved it. I loved her!

We were inseparable. I had never dated, much less had I ever felt so strongly about someone. I was never cool, but with her I felt that way. She made me a better version of myself. I was never confident, but with her I was comfortable in my own skin. Every time I made her giggle; I fell deeper in love with every sound that she would make. Every time she would touch me; the rest of the world would melt away. It melted away for her too.

She would watch me compete every chance that she got. Whether competing on the lanes or in life in general, she would yell and cheer for me on my good days. I could collapse into her arms, and she would hold me and rub the back of my head on my bad days. She was everything that I never knew that I needed.

~ *All You Need is Love...Kind of* ~

Time passed and we spent more and more time together. I got a decent job and now have a steady income making decent money. My best friend's father got me a job delivering medicine to pharmacies and bringing bank paperwork back to the Federal Reserve Monday through Friday. This schedule meant that I could still bowl regionals on the weekends. This also afforded me the opportunity to get my own apartment. This was a touchy subject for my parents, especially my mother.

My mother viewed me moving out, at 21, mind you, as losing her son. Misty was the catalyst in her mind that fueled that reaction. They began to argue during nearly every interaction. No amount of persuading was going to change my mind. I got my own place. A place where Misty and I could be alone. No arguing with parents, just us being us. We were young, in love and dreaming about building our future together. Still hanging on to our virginities by a thread. We started making that small one-bedroom apartment a home.

I worked hard, but didn't mind it. She was living with her grandmother a few miles from my apartment. Her grandmother covered for us and Misty would stay with me for days at a time. The feeling of waking up and seeing the love of my life and getting to hold her as I fell asleep was the greatest thing in the world. Our usual date locales involved Northwest Expressway in OKC, but that wouldn't do for a special date. I took her to Edmond.

~ *Waterworks* ~

We had spoken informally about spending our lives together, but nothing official, yet. We went somewhere on a date, I don't remember the location. The reason being is that the location never really mattered. If I had her hand in mine, I was exactly where I wanted to be. Our date ended at Hafer Park in Edmond. I walked with her hand in hand to a deck that oversaw a duck pond. I told her that I loved her, for the tenth time that day. I just got to the point where I apologized for the habit, but I couldn't help it. When I felt it, I would say it and I felt it constantly. I reached into my pocket and dropped to my knee. I will never forget her gasping and smiling. I said, "Misty, will you complete my life and be my wife?" She giggled and said yes with tears streaming down her face.

We set the date for December 20th, only a couple months away. For those keeping track, virginities are still intact! This, however, is when so many forces began to work on me to not marry the love of my life. Not the least of which was my mother. She was certain that Misty would break my heart and that she would leave me. Even our preacher pressured me to postpone if I had a single solitary doubt. I made one of the worst decisions of my life, I told Misty that I wanted to postpone. I broke her heart and mine in the same moment. I hated myself for making her cry. I hated myself for not protecting her from the pain, the pain that I caused. We broke up.

Each day crept by like an eternity. I didn't want to do anything that usually brought me joy. She became such a central facet of everything that I enjoyed, so much so that everywhere that I looked for happiness, all that I saw was that she was not there. I was miserable, then I got asked out on a date.

I had dated this woman for a while during one of the times that Misty and I had broken up a couple years prior. She was experienced. I was still innocent. This girl wanted to be my first. She flat told me so on the phone. She asked to come see me, I agreed. We had the apartment to ourselves. She pressed her lips and her body against mine, but I turned her down. It didn't feel right for me, so it wouldn't have been right for us to proceed. I wasn't over Misty. There was nothing wrong with this woman, she just wasn't Misty. The gentleman that ended up with her would be beyond lucky to have her. My heart, however, belonged to Misty and no one else. I had to get her back.

~Time? What Time? ~

Months had passed, but you would never have known it. Our guards were down instantly, we once again fell hard and fast! I was going to try and buy a home, a double wide trailer, I know-I know, "nothing but the best Clark!" I didn't care and she didn't care either. It was going to be ours and that is all that mattered. I was driving quite a bit for work. I would start at 8am and go until 8pm. I would drive to her mom's house often before work and after work just to hold her for a few minutes. It was worth every mile, worth every minute to feel the touch that made the rest of the world melt away.

Once again, I was begged by my mother not to marry her. I was cut off financially as a result, but I didn't care. I wasn't going to let her go again. Come what may, we were going to take on the world, together. Things were better than they had ever been. I was going to show her just how much I truly cared for her. I offered to make her dinner and asked her to come to my apartment. She readily agreed.

She wouldn't know until years later that I sat at my bedroom window and waited to see her cross the courtyard of the apartment complex. I was on the third floor. I cannot remember how many roses I bought. There were rose petals on every stair, rose petals leading to the dining room table and leading to and onto the bed. We had never made love before, but somehow, we both knew that it was time. The smile on her face when I opened the door once again set my body on fire. The tenderness in her gaze. The trust that we had for each other. The oneness that we had craved for so long to share with ourselves and no one else, was nothing short of a fairytale. The innocence was adorable. The chemistry was undeniable and would remain unmatched for the rest of our lives. She would tremble and giggle when I touched and kissed her body, just as I would when she touched and kissed mine. It was symbolic of the ecstasy that rewards two souls that are meant to be together when they finally get the opportunity to become one.

After what felt like an eternity and immediate simultaneously, the moment had arrived. We had heard stories about how painful it would be for her, and it worried me so much. I did not want to hurt her, ever. I entered her slowly while kissing her. She gasped and froze. I panicked and asked if she was okay! She looked me in the eyes, grinned and said, "just don't move." To this day, it is the purest and sweetest memory that I have of us. We did not experience any of the awfulness that so many do. We were absolutely made for each other. There was no pain when I did move. We experienced pleasure, ecstasy, but most of all, we experienced love.

We would lose count of how many times that we made love. We started on Friday night and continued through Sunday. Seemingly the only breaks that we took were for me to walk to the corner store for more condoms while she would sit in a cold tub to reduce swelling so we could continue again and again. We made only one trip together out of the apartment for take-out. We were completely wrapped up in each other, exploring each other and loving each other. We had hours of passion mixed with giggling and talking about our dreams of taking on the world together. We loved each other more than we thought was humanly possible. It was possible though, at least for us it was. It was the most perfect thing that I would ever know. She was the love of my life, and I was hers.

~Building a Life Together ~

Misty made me feel more alive than I had ever felt in my life. I was desperately in love with her. I had waited so long to give my heart to someone. I did not date like my peers. I felt no need, until I found her. I gave her all of me and in return, she gave all of herself to me. She was the most perfect thing that I had ever had the privilege of being around. Nearly everyone I knew said don't do it, but the world didn't matter. She was the love of my life and that was the only thing that mattered to me. The resistance was fierce, especially from my mother. She was convinced that Misty would destroy me eventually. She told me flat out that we would last 6 months. I just couldn't see Misty hurting me. The world didn't know her like I did. I loved her with every piece of my soul. I was going to marry the woman of my dreams and there was nothing in the world that could stop me.

There would be no grand wedding, but neither of us cared. All that we cared about was each other. The wedding was the absolute definition of spur of the moment. I worked that morning. We then made phone calls to alert the family that we would be married by the Justice of the Peace that afternoon. No fancy decorations, no fancy attire, no pomp and circumstance, no honeymoon, just simply two people who loved each other more than anything on Earth. She wore a sunflower dress, and I wore slacks and a polo shirt. She was so beautiful. I truly felt like the luckiest man on planet Earth. I felt complete for the first time in my life.

~Cutting to the Chase ~

Now here's where the timeline gets tricky. You get to read privileged information. Information that would not be made known to me for decades. Two conversations over haircuts. Two haircuts, one for my brother-in-law and one for my brother from another mother, Chris.

As stated earlier, my mother was a second-generation barber, not a stylist, not a hairdresser, but a traditional barber. The antique Koken barber chairs in her shop were the same ones I sat in as a child when my grandfather ran the shop. The hard red leather as cold and unforgiving as the old man that built and destroyed that business before my mother resurrected it.

My best friend sat in that chair after I married Misty. My mother, wielding clippers, made him take a vow. She made him vow to be there for me. He was confused, he was always there for me. She was serious. Dead serious. "When it falls apart, he will need you. You must promise to be there for him. He is going to be lost and hurt worse than he can imagine. I don't think I will be here. Promise me that you'll be there for him." He said of course. She added, "just this one, after the others he will be okay, but when he loses Misty, he will need you. After that, you are off the hook." He agreed and shook his head as we all did whenever she spoke of her early Earthly exit prophecies over the years.

My brother-in-law also got one of those chats. The subject matter was similar in ways, but different. She blamed herself, yet in a way she blamed me. She told him that the marriage wouldn't last. She still claimed that Misty wasn't the right one for me, but that wasn't the reason it wouldn't work. She said, "he will fail at this marriage. I didn't raise him for it. She'd have to love him more than he loves her. Not equal, not even just a bit more, but a lot more. It will fail. His marriage won't survive. He will marry again, it will fail. Maybe over and over, I don't know if he will ever find the person he needs. It is how he's made. It is how I made him. He is not mean; he just needs someone exceptional to be there for him when he needs them."

~Starting our life ~

We started our life together in that double wide trailer. Blissfully unaware of our humble beginnings, only aware of our love for each other. It was enough for us, more than enough. We didn't even recognize the "things" that we didn't possess, because we were so content that we possessed each other. We had been together for years at that point, but you would never have known it. We were still exploring everything about each other. There were more magical moments than could be counted. Sharing our dinners together, cuddling on the couch, cuddling in bed, cuddling no matter where we were, literally everywhere we were. We had been together for years but simply could not keep our hands off each other. It was amazing, I had a wife, a lover and best friend all wrapped into one person. She was my copilot.

~ 500 Miles ~

I was driving for a living, close to 500 miles per day, while chasing my dream of bowling. She was my literal copilot then as well. Miles upon miles driven comprise some of my favorite memories with Misty. We got up at 4am together to go on my route. She never complained about lost sleep and as newlyweds, we lost quite a bit. She would ride with me, day in and day out. I was earning a living for us and getting to hold her hand all day. I was getting to tell her stories and share our hopes and dreams for our future. We didn't interact with many other people, but we didn't miss it. We had each other and that was enough for us. We woke up early and made love late into the night. My family was still weary, still warning, but we completed each other and that's all that we cared about. It is all that registered with us as important. We were misunderstood by some, but to us, we were perfect. We were perfect until we weren't. It wasn't even our fault. We didn't see it coming, nobody did.

~That one. That One Right There ~

I went to war with my parents over Misty. She knew of some of the battles that I engaged in on our behalf, but nowhere near the entirety of the wounds that were inflicted on both sides. My mother and I were very much alike. We fought hard. We fought dirty. We fought to inflict emotional pain. I shielded Misty from as much as I possibly could in hopes that if I did, that one day, it would all get better. In hopes that my parents would see her just as I did all this time, the best thing that had ever happened to me. The battles continued.

I was born with the ability to cut people to shreds with my words. It got to the point with my mother that I no longer held back, she didn't either. She swore that Misty was out to destroy me. She saw Misty becoming just like her mother. She was afraid that Misty didn't truly love me. She was afraid that I would simply be the first father to her children, that I would soon be an ex-husband forever tied to her by our shared progeny. I lashed back in every hurtful way that I could imagine. My mother wept frantically when she couldn't convince me one evening. I told her that I was done and not to reach out anymore. She replied that she wouldn't take care of herself if we didn't stay in touch. I told her that that was on her, not me and that it wasn't fair.

I will never forget my father yelling at me in their living room saying, "get out, you are killing my wife, and I will no longer allow it!" My response, "So you don't want me to have a life of my own, I will just kill myself if I can't keep her as my wife!" Dramatic? Yes, but my mother was not to be out done. She lashed back saying, "I will kill myself too and that way we can be buried together." I was unphased. I did not have a child. I had no comprehension of the fear and panic that a parent can feel for their child. Without hesitation, I said the most horrible thing that I would ever say to another human being in my life, "bury me on top, so the last thing I can do is shit on you!" She went silent. The room fell silent. I stood there, still seething with anger. My father, his shoulders dropped as he calmly walked over to me. He held my shoulders, looked me in the eyes and said, "that one, that one right there, you'll regret that one for the rest of your life one day." He was right.

A couple of weeks passed by and once again we all ended up at my parents' house. I cannot remember the specific cause of the argument. I do recall being in my parent's driveway. The argument, no doubt, had its origins in my mother's mistrust of Misty, much like the other altercations over the past couple years. This time was different. This time was worse. Insults were hurled back and forth. For some reason we were all sitting in the same vehicle, I cannot recall why. My mother hurled her best insult at Misty. My mother lost to no one in verbal altercations, except for me. Today however, Misty would one up her. Misty's reply? "Oh yeah, well I fuck your son every night!" There was no comeback for that. My mother became enraged and lunged for Misty. She missed, narrowly. In a flash, my father pulled my mother out of the car. Over her cries, I heard him say, "now he has his excuse, now we have lost him!" He was right.

I remember pulling out of the driveway, numb in disbelief of what had just happened. I remember driving away from their house. The rest is an absolute haze of bewilderment. I knew things had changed in an instant. There was no more defending her actions. There was no more rationalizing her thought processes. My mother had lunged at my wife. There was no going back. I looked at Misty and said I choose you. At least that is what I think happened. If I didn't say it out loud, I promised myself that I would choose Misty. How could I not? She was the love of my life. I would distance myself from my parents from that point forward. I would cling to Misty, my love, to our love. It was enough all by itself.

Months passed by without interacting with my parents. It was just easier that way. It was easier on me. It was easier on Misty, and I imagined that it was easier on my folks. Misty and I went on about our lives. I was young, 22, and I simply enjoyed the calmness. There had been so much unsolicited input for so long, that quietness was a welcome change of pace. Perhaps with the forced cooling off period mom would come around and realize that what Misty and I had was going to last. In the meantime, I enjoyed my wife. We continued our journey of exploration. Without the outside interruptions we dove deeper into our marriage and explored each other emotionally. It was smooth. It was easy. It was effortless just as it always had been. It was simple. I had even decided to quit driving for a living and get back to working in bowling alleys to chase my dream more seriously. Misty was onboard as always. She believed in me, even more than I believed in myself. Our destiny was calling, but it wasn't what we thought it was going to be. As it often can, the simple ringing of a phone can change, well, everything.

~ *Rooftop Recollections and the Unanswered Call* ~

My phone rang one morning. The Caller ID showed that it was my mother. She hadn't tried to call me in quite some time. I wasn't in the mood to argue. I wasn't in the mood for a guilt trip. I picked up the phone and hung it up without even hearing her voice. I left the phone off the hook and left the house. It was my final day driving for a living. My deliveries took me through my hometown where my folks lived. I drove on the road behind their house. I can remember glancing at the roof of their house as I drove by that morning. I remembered how I would call before leaving the bowling center on my late shifts. I'd work till 2am on the weekends and I would take her order for Taco Bell. She'd wait up on me and we would eat our late-night meal together. Her with her Cheesarito and me with my tacos. It used to be so much easier before I found love. We never went to war. Sure, we argued, but never was it a war. I missed those days of talking about me going on tour. I missed it dearly.

I remember making my last delivery that evening. I remember turning in my badge to the delivery company. I was excited to be done. I was excited to be going back to work at my home bowling center the next morning. It felt like everything was once again falling into place.

I walked in the front door of the trailer with a grin as I was greeted by Misty. We curled up on the couch and started watching Allie Mcbeal. The phone rang, I didn't answer it on purpose. It rang several more times before I begrudgingly answered it. My grandmother was on the other end of the line. She said that I needed to get to the hospital quick because mom wasn't doing well. My grandmother wanted me to pick her up on our way to the hospital.

I knew exactly what mom was up to and I was going to let her have it when we got to the hospital. It was all just for attention. That was all that it was, and I knew it. She wasn't taking care of her diabetes so that I would have to come around. That way she could guilt me into leaving Misty. I told Misty my thoughts and she too agreed with my assessment of the situation. I would arrive and tell my mother that she HAD to take care of herself whether I was in her life or not. Yup, I had it all planned out down to the conceited tone that I would use to get my point across to this stubborn woman. We arrived at an empty house at my grandmother's home. Someone else must have gotten her. Thinking not much of it, we made our way to the hospital.

~ Room 419 Just Around the Corner ~

We arrived at the hospital, and I went to the information desk. I was greeted by a girl that I went to high school with just a few years prior. I asked her what room my mother was in, 419. Misty and I got on the elevator, and I was still seething with anger over mom ruining our evening with more of her antics. We didn't say anything to each other on the elevator. She just squeezed my hand in assurance that I was doing the right thing, that I was justified.   We had both had our fill of the drama. We stepped out of the elevator and followed the signs to find room 419. We were approaching a corner when we heard a woman screaming "no, no, no!" I looked at Misty and said, "my God someone just died."

As we turned the corner, I began to recognize faces. The faces of my entire family. It was my family that was weeping in disbelief. My eyes settled on my sister, she was the origin of the scream of no, no, God no. We locked eyes and she said only two words, mom's dead. I screamed and asked how long she had been gone. I screamed that I had made an extra stop to pick up my grandmother. My cousin started to explain that she had coded a while ago, but I barely waited for an answer, I let go of Misty's hand and turned my back on everyone, including Misty. I almost ran down the hallway. I can remember Misty crying out, "don't leave me!" I was so distraught that I couldn't even turn back toward her.

She chased me to the stairwell. I was in absolute hysterics. Nurses also followed me into the stairwell, where I collapsed. I cried uncontrollably. Misty held me against her chest. I barely knew where I was at. I remember screaming, "my God what have I done!" I remember a nurse saying that it was going to be okay and that she was so sorry. I was crying so hard that my nose was bleeding all over Misty's jacket. I looked at the nurse and said, "you don't understand, I hung up on her today. I hung up on her when she called. I didn't even say hello to my mom on the day she died!" The nurse gasped and covered her mouth, physically admitting that she couldn't imagine the pain and regret that I felt at that moment. What could she say, there were no words.

~ The Reason for The Call ~

I would later hear the dreadful story of her day as relayed by my sister. She was a diabetic and stress was not her friend. This caused her to spiral in respect to her diabetes. She woke up on her final day hallucinating because of the early stages of diabetic ketoacidosis. She had been sick for days. She was dehydrated from diarrhea and vomiting. This exacerbated everything. She began hallucinating.

The hallucinations were demonic in nature. The demons forbade her to call for help. The demons told her if she called anyone, that person would die. She not only thought she was dying. She was certain of it. She knew that I would never forgive myself if she passed while we were on bad terms. Against the demon's wishes, she called me. It took her hours to summon the courage to make the call. That was when I saw her number on the caller ID. That was when I simply hung up my phone before even hearing my mother's voice for what would have been the last time and left for work. She would not attempt another call.

My father would call her each day at lunch. She didn't answer at the barber shop or at home that day. So, he rushed home to check on her. She was incoherent and my father called 911. She was taken to the hospital by ambulance. She eventually got stabilized at the hospital and was doing better later in the day. The funny thing is that I drove by the hospital not knowing she was there that day. I could literally see the window of the room that she was in that day, never knowing that she was recounting the horrors of her morning. Never knowing that she was asking why her baby boy hadn't shown up to visit her yet. When she asked where I was, my family told her that they called me and that I couldn't make it until later. She wanted to see her son, to make sure that I was okay. It was a close call, and she wanted to fix things. However, they hadn't called me, but rather they were afraid that we would argue and that I would worsen her condition. My sister told me that mom had stabilized and told my sister, "I think I'm going to be alright." Only to start gasping for air just a few minutes later. My sister got to witness my mother begging the nurses to save her life. That is when I received the call to get to the hospital.

~ Gravity ~

I remember Misty helping me to my feet in that hospital stairwell. Seeing her covered in my blood, seeing my blood on the floor, I stumbled to a bathroom to wash my face. With nurses and orderlies following close behind I lost it again. I screamed at myself in the bathroom mirror. So enraged at my own ego that I took my frustrations out on the paper towel dispenser, gashing open my bowling hand. I didn't care. Bowling was her dream too and it seemed to not matter as much now, if she didn't get to see me accomplish it. My hand wrapped in bloody gauze; I made my way back up the stairs to find my father. How in the world was I going to face my father. He had told me that I was killing her, and he was right. I braced myself as I walked toward this shattered man. A man that had just lost the love of his life. My Superman leaned against the wall. If not for that wall, I am not sure that he would've had the strength to remain upright.

As I approached him, there seemed to be more gravity. It was literally harder to move. As if not only the gravity of the situation was hitting me, but also as if grief and shame was tethering me to the planet. The force felt so immense that my voice cracked as I said, "daddy." I had not called him daddy since I was a toddler, but that was all that I could utter in that moment. That is what I felt in that moment. I felt small, scared and insignificant. He didn't acknowledge me. I was crushed. I had lost both parents at the same moment. My sister nudged him.

He was so consumed by grief, reeling in his own despair that he didn't hear me. He reached for me and said my God, my son and he wrapped his arms around me. I absolutely lost it and kept saying I'm so sorry daddy in between my bellows of regret. When I finally let go of him, he saw my hand bleeding through the gauze. He asked what had happened and I told him. He told me that I couldn't mess up my ticket. The doctor interrupted us and asked if he wanted an autopsy done. He said no, that he didn't want her cut up any more than necessary. He couldn't bear the thought of it.

I had chosen Misty over my mother. The gravity of that choice I had been completely fine with, a choice that now haunted my every thought. Everyone knew the burden to which I shackled myself, especially Misty. She would have front row seats to the end of my world, to the end of us. I would cry myself to sleep for months. My father was right. I wanted those words back. Worse than that, he was right about something else, I had killed her. I was the one that caused her stress. I denied her access to her son. I hurt her as deeply as I possibly could as often as I could.

~ *The Journey TO Rest* ~

Losing a loved one is always tragic but having to plan a funeral from zero to tombstone while reeling in despair is cataclysmic. My mother had 'seen' this coming for years but hadn't planned anything in terms of her final arrangements. We DID know a small portion of her wishes. She forbade us from spending a large amount of money on her casket. She had always told us to pick the cheapest one available. We made our way through the gallery of caskets and asked where the cheapest one was located. It was hideous and none of us could picture it as her final resting place. I said, "how about the second cheapest?" It still wasn't perfect, but I could see her pursing her lips in my mind's eye as the tally crept upwards in dollars. So, a glittery brown casket with a mallard on the inside with the words, fly away home would have to do.

I tried desperately to hold it together as my father was an absolute wreck and rightfully so.   In fact, it was if we took turns falling apart in front of each other. I would break down and then suddenly I would feel as if I had a warm blanket wrapped around me. In those moments of warmness, my gaze would fix upon my father, who would undoubtedly start to crumble before my very eyes. I truly feel that it was my mother attempting to comfort us, one at a time. We kept her busy as we were frantically trying to put her funeral together.

Misty was, as always, by my side. She was at the funeral home and cried with me and my family. I was so tormented with my own regret, so fixated on myself that it didn't even register how hard it had to be on her. To be the one that everyone thought came between my mother and me. I did not hate her. I never could. I never will. However, there was a change in our dynamic. It was instant. It was my fault. I hated myself for it.

Misty held me as I cried at the funeral. My body was just limp. It didn't even feel like I had a form or shape anymore. She would hold my hands, covered in tears and snot, she would hold my hands. She was frantic, I couldn't see it at the time, but she too was heartbroken and fearful. I couldn't see it at the time, but I was destroyed because I had not just lost my mother, but I had lost Misty in those same moments. It is not that she wasn't there. You see when I look back at our world as it was crumbling, I can see something different. I can see her reaching for my hand as she always had. Trying to fill in the cracks in the walls of our relationship, to shore up our foundation as we begin to lose our footing. It was precious to her, and she was doing this while carrying the burden of my mother's passing. I remember her reaching, I didn't see it at the time, but she was reaching for me. I don't remember reaching for her. I hate myself for that. Then one day, when we were in the car she confessed to me her fear.

We were sitting at a stoplight at 33rd and Broadway. She told me that she was afraid of something. She started crying. When I asked her what she was afraid of she replied, "I am afraid that you're never going to laugh again, I'm afraid that I've lost you." I didn't reply. I had no reply that would make her feel better. I didn't think that I would ever be the same again. I didn't think that we would ever be the same again. I was right, we never would.

~ Calm ~

Misty still supported my dreams, just as she always had. Even though we were weathering everything that came with mom's passing, she still wanted my dream for me, and I never thanked her for that. I felt a strong urge to compete at the highest level. Those closest to me knew I could not live with myself if I didn't go for it. Now that my mother was gone, there was no one that understood that better than Misty. I felt like I owed it to my mother to try and compete against the best on the planet. I had never even gotten close to earning a check on the national tour. My previous attempts at the national level were dismal at best. There was no logical reason for me to do it at this point. I hadn't even been practicing like I should. There was no rational conversation in my home that was had between myself and Misty. Instead, it was a passionate kiss, a hug, a wink and a "go get them baby." With that influx of energy from her, I was headed off to attempt to do just that.

I was still an unknown in terms of professional bowling on the national tour. I arrived with my father in tow, to compete for the first time since my mother's passing. He looked as nervous as I should have felt. Here's the thing, I wasn't nervous, and I was always nervous. Perhaps I was still too emotionally drained, still numb from losing my mother. The competition started and it was just me, at least that's what it felt like. After the first day of competition against 220 of the best players on the planet, I was 10th, this nobody was in 10th. I was in disbelief. My first call was to Misty. She was almost always there to watch me compete, but she had to work. I loved to hear her voice. I could hear how happy she was for me. I was excited, but cautiously optimistic as I had 2 more days of qualifying to go before making the top 24 for match play. Before I knew it, I was starting day 2 and I knew there was no way I could hold on to 10th place. I didn't hold on…

Day two of the competition commenced and I was still calm. I crossed pairs with another no-name player in my region and he began getting excited for me. It looked like the first block wasn't a total fluke. It was as if I was all alone again. I wasn't worried about anything. I didn't check the leader board, not because I was cocky, but it simply never occurred to me. As round 2 ended, I was no longer in 10th. I had moved up to fourth. Now it was getting interesting…

Day three of the competition started and still I was calm, calmer than I had ever been in my life. The round flew by at a blistering pace and before I knew it, I was in my final game. Now I was nervous. Now I started missing. I missed shots over and over. I could feel it slipping away. I could hear the words that I would have to say to Misty. I could hear the pain that would be present in her voice. I could see the tears in my father's eyes. I just had 7 frames to go, and I couldn't hold on to it. I felt a lump in my throat, but then someone grabbed me by the shoulders. I couldn't believe who gripped my drooping shoulders.

It was a multi-time titlist, Brian Himmler. His nickname was the chief. He said, "dude, you can miss every shot the rest of the way out and you will still make match play, just relax and enjoy it!" I did exactly that. I immediately started striking and finished strong. I ended up in 10th place. I collapsed into my father's arms and we both cried. I had my best qualifying ever at the time that I needed it the most. We wiped away our tears and just grinned at each other. Neither said it out loud, but we both felt that mom had to be helping me a bit. Then what we heard next caught us both by surprise.

~ A Mother's Pride ~

We heard the tour director call for "Stoney Pride, report to the PBA Pressroom please." My father and I looked at each other with amazement. I was about to be interviewed. They wanted to interview me, a nobody.

I made my way to the pressroom and was called over to the newspaper sports writers' area. I was asked about my regional titles…of which I had none, Team USA experience…I had none, big amateur tournament wins…I had none. Then with a look of bewilderment they asked, "well, what in the world do you attribute your sudden ability to compete with the best on the planet?? New ball contract??" I told them that I had just lost my mother suddenly, no great details of the underlying tragedy beyond the obvious. I simply told them that this was the calmest that I had ever been and that this one was for her. The next morning held my first match play appearance, but it also held something else completely unexpected.

I walked in to start match play and found my starting lane assignment. There were some superstars in the top 24, I was starting off against a good player, not a superstar. However, there were a ton of people behind my pair of lanes. I walked to get some water and heard someone say, "that's him, that's Stoney Pride!" I was confused. A fellow regional player Tony Franklin motioned for me to come over to him. He was about to clear up my confusion.

He handed me a copy of the Dallas Morning News and there was a massive write-up about someone that most people had never heard of before. It was over me and my mother. It was titled "A Mother's Pride."

This is why "I" had a gallery. This is why I had people cheering for me when I was nowhere near the top of the field. It was simply amazing. An amazing escape for a week. A gift from a son to a mother and from a mother to her son. I know she saw it. I know she had a little something to do with it too. I finished 16th that week. That would be my highest finish ever and I couldn't dream of a better situation in which for it to happen. That day I was the 16th best player in the world. I was signing autographs that day. The next day, if you bowled in Edmond, Oklahoma, I was making $7.00/hour and I was asking you what size bowling shoes you needed. Back to reality I went.

~ Driven...Apart ~

I eventually went back to driving for a living. The money was better, and you never seem to have enough of that. Misty was working harder than ever. We saw each other less and less. It hurt me and I know it hurt her as well. I began working two routes, my days spanned from 4am to 8:30pm for a while. I was drifting farther from my dream and farther from Misty. I came up with a plan to fix it.

I decided to open my own business, a pro-shop. I learned that trade at the age of 16 and knew the business as well as a

22-year-old possibly could. I quit my afternoon route and ran my shop from 1pm to 8pm after I got done running my morning delivery route. My hours of work were not any shorter, but it would be time better spent. Misty wanted to be a part of my shop, to be a team, as we should have been. I did not have the funds to start the shop, my father co-signed the note to get me started. This was March 1999, 3 months after mom's passing. I could still hear her warnings echoing in my head. This was the last thing that my father was going to be able to do for me financially. Mom was worried that Misty would destroy me one day, if I gave her control over my shop would I be giving her the tools to do just that?

I would never find that out. I kept something separate from Misty for the first time. It hurt her. I didn't realize at the time just how much so. We had our fights before mom passed, usually over nothing. To be honest, I cannot recall any real reason that we ever had problems before mom passed away. It didn't matter, we always made up. We both enjoyed that. It seemed that every fight we had, once we made up, we were stronger for it. The love was deeper, it was truer. But now it was different, at least for me. We weren't stronger after each argument we were farther apart each time. Not out of hatred or resentment, I could never hate her. I would always love her. I would love her endlessly. I got to the point that I hated myself where she was concerned. I hated myself for the "choice" that I had made. Not for choosing her, but for failing as a negotiator. I should have tried harder to build a bridge between her and my mother. I could have fixed it and had them both in my life. But instead, I lost my mother and the love of my life on the same day. That was what was destroying me, and I couldn't figure out how to fix it. I couldn't get past it. I was failing the love of my life.

I don't remember our last argument. How sad is that? I left the trailer and called my best friend. He and his wife's solution was to take my mind off Misty. They gave me some alcohol and took me to a club. I watched them dance. I watched them stare at each other. I was hit on. I politely said no thank you to puzzled faces. I don't remember much, but I curled up in a ball in a corner booth and ugly cried in public over Misty. I was not over her. I could never get over her. I would never get over her. I was in no shape to drive and passed out at Chris' house. I left in the morning to fix things with Misty.

I got home to find her gone. I got home to find a note. A note that explained that my failure to return home over night was a clear message that I didn't want to be with her anymore. I called her and she repeated the note's contents and confirmed that it was over for her. I was broken, utterly broken. I gave her space for a couple weeks, then I called her again.

I asked how she was doing; she said she was doing well. That she said that she enjoyed going out to clubs and dancing. It destroyed me. I begged her to come home. I begged for forgiveness. She refused. I filed for divorce and filed for bankruptcy. Divorced and bankrupt at 23. After meeting her with the divorce papers, I would not see her face nor hear her voice again for years. I had truly lost the love of my life. I let her go, because I loved her. Where would I go from here?

~ A Rumor? About Me? ~

I threw myself into work. I was driving in the mornings and delivering pharmaceuticals, then in the afternoons and evenings I ran my pro shop. The days were still 16-17 hours long, but I had nothing or no one else to occupy my time so it didn't matter any longer. I got home from one of those long days and my phone rang, it was my best friend, Chris.

He told me to come to Meridian Lanes in Oklahoma City. I really didn't want to go, but he seemed insistent, so I obliged. I walked in and said hi to all the familiar faces. The bowling community is tight knit, so everyone knew that I was divorced and bankrupt. I got the sympathetic "poor guy" stares from just about everyone in the building. I leaned against the wall watching Chris bowl. I hated that bowling center for some reason. It was notorious for being easy, nicknamed the house of scores. Luck never seemed to be on my side there. However, that night would be an exception. I heard a female voice call my name. This was going to be trouble. I could feel it.

I walked over to where she was sitting. She asked for me to lean over and she whispered into my ear, "I heard that you are single now." In my best Doc Holliday, I replied, "that's the rumor." She laughed and said, "well I can fix that." We started talking a little bit. I had seen her around before. She was mischievous. She was a handful. She was a different kind of fun. She walked out of the center with Chris and me. She jumped on my back, and I flung her over my shoulder, and I asked if she was hungry. She looked confused that someone actually asked if SHE needed something. We went to IHOP and had pancakes at midnight. She distracted me from the pain that I felt dally. The pain that still lingered from losing Misty. I dove into that beautiful pool of distraction headfirst.

~ Sultry Sidekick ~

She bowled a lot. That was another point of attraction. She threw the ball well. As odd as it may seem, to me that was sexy in and of itself. If I was at the bowling alley, so was she. She seemed to like that I was in the "popular crowd" at this point. I didn't care to be popular. It's funny that once you stop giving a shit whether you are liked or not, then people start to like you, it's weird. I was kind to her, nobody else had really done that for her. Sex happened quickly, but that was not the greatest source of chemistry. Looking back, we were more friends than anything. We got along exceptionally well, just not in a super passionate, can't keep our hands each other sort of way. I was not her first. So that bond would not be duplicated either. Her parents were great and supported me in every way that they could. We would marry within mere months on my birthday.

We moved into my parent's old house as my father remarried quickly after my mother's passing. It was smooth sailing for a while. No fights, no drama, just hanging out and going bowling. I closed my pro shop, as I couldn't compete with the other guys selling stuff below cost just to drive me out of business. That was a hard day, but I took a job working desk at my home bowling alley and continued to try to compete on the regional tour. Then, once again life would change the itinerary of my existence with no notice.

~ *Fighting Weight* ~

I injured my knee and had to have what was supposed to be simple surgery. When I woke up from anesthesia, the surgeon was just shaking his head. He told me that in his 20 years of cutting on knees, mine was the worst that he had ever seen. He said that my bowling career was over. I quit and took a manager position at the alley and remapped my future.

I weighed 267 pounds, the worst shape of my life. I had to stand in a bowling center and not do what I loved, throw a bowling ball. My knee healed as much as it was going to, and I tried to throw a shot one night after close. I collapsed in pain in the third step of my five-step approach. I was devastated! Was it over? Could I come up with a way around it?

Even then, I understood the basic physics of how all that extra weight put pressure on my knee. So, I set the goal of getting the weight off. I thought that at 240, I might be able to tolerate the pain. I joined a gym and began my affair with an elliptical machine and went back to a subway diet that Misty and I had done years before. In two months, I was down to 240. I grabbed my bowling equipment out of the closet and after closing the center one night, I would once again see if I could manage to do what I loved.

Once again, I got to my third step and faltered, but did not collapse. It was progress, slow going, but it was progress, nonetheless. I had to get to 220. I continued my affair with the elliptical. Now I am upping my cardiovascular interludes to two hours a day. In another month, I had made it to 220. I once again grabbed my stuff out of the closet and headed to the center. Once again, I faltered. It was better still, but still incredibly painful. Maybe the doc was right, but I wasn't ready to give up just yet. I now set my eyes on 202 pounds, why 202 pounds? That was Rocky's fighting weight, but if you are a true Rocky fan, you already knew that didn't you? I had less to lose overall, it took me two months, but I hit 202 and headed to attempt to practice.

~ Chasing it Again ~

I did not falter, it didn't hurt. I was lean. I was hungry for competition. I began practicing two times a day. I was working full time managing the alley, but also simultaneously starting to chase my dream again. I got my pro card back and started entering regionals again. I began cashing at nearly every event and making match play regularly. I was then approached by my first sponsor. I quit my job and concentrated on practicing for the national tour, my life-long dream was within my grasp. I had 2 months to prepare. Those months flew by.

My marriage was in good shape, or so I thought, when I left for my first 7 tour stops. Week one was awful. Out of 120 players, I finished 110th. It was embarrassing. I had drilled a bunch of new equipment before leaving and went with a different manufacturer than I usually threw. I was distraught. I was angry. I was terrified of letting my first real chance to make my dreams come true slip through my fingers. I called the warehouse in Dallas and let them know I was driving from Wichita to hand pick a couple of my old favorite bowling balls, the V2 by Ebonite. I looked through hundreds to get 2 with the specs I wanted and hit a shop in OKC to drill them and then headed to stop number two, Kansas City.

I crushed the Kansas City tournament. Making my first match play appearance on the National Tour in 4 years. I qualified 4th for match play and ended up 16th. I was living my dream. I called to tell my wife about my finish. She was a bit colder than I thought she would be. But not as cold as she would be a few days later.

~ Tired ~

My phone rang, it was my wife. I was in a good mood, fresh off the best performance of my career. I was literally living the dream. She told me that she was tired. I asked if she had been sleeping alright. She said, "I am tired of you. I want a divorce." She didn't like being alone. I couldn't blame her for that. In my mind, accurate or not, I believe that she wanted me to quit, to give up on my dream for her, for us. My reply? "Drive the divorce papers to the state-line and I will meet you there tonight, that way I can make it to the Memphis Stop in the morning." She met me there as agreed at around 10pm. I will never forget her smile. I wasn't certain if it was a smile of relief or that smile that people get when they are in an uncomfortable situation, a coping mechanism of sorts. She wasn't IN love with me. I am not sure that she ever really was. On that drive to Memphis, I realized that I was never really IN love with her either, but we did love each other. She's a good human, no doubt about that. In retrospect, I believe that we were good friends. Two people that needed to find each other while they were trying to find themselves. She would check in on me from time to time over the years as I would her, as friends do.

I simply made my way to finish the last 5 stops of my tour swing. I was focused, yet free. No one to update except my sponsor and my best friend. I made match play again quickly. I remember sitting at a table with a couple of tour players as the results rolled in showing that I easily made it to match play yet again and I got asked a question. Did you get divorced last week? I said, yup. Their reply, way to bounce back bro.

~ Bye-Bye Birdy ~

The rest of the swing went well, but not well enough. It was always something. Something bizarre, something heartbreaking, but this time it was beyond anything that I could imagine. I missed cashing in events by a single pin more times than I can count, but this ONE event, this one Mr. Destiny moment took the cake.

It goes like this; tournaments last a week from start to finish. People will pay to come in and watch the best of the best competing throughout the week. As you can imagine, as it gets closer to the television finals, more and more people come in to watch the action. They were moving in more seating for the fans and had a door propped open. It made for a little more noise, but we are professionals and can handle stuff like that. I was in the hunt and bowling decent when the universe would throw something unexpected my way.

As I made my approach to shoot a ten-pin spare, a bird flew directly in front of me. This happened at the apex of my swing. I shut down my swing and wrenched my back. I had never withdrawn from a tournament before. I had 3 games to go and decided to finish out the block. It was excruciating, all the while my mind was racing at the odds of this miraculous mishap. The sheer odds of it blew my mind, just as it blew my chances of finishing the swing. I had to call my sponsor and break the news

~ How's That for a Sign ~

The 'good' players on the tour stayed in nice hotels. Myself, however? I was bowling on a budget. I stayed with Tom Bodett. Afterall he always left the light on for me. So, as I was searching for the wisdom of whether I should try to finish the swing injured or tell my sponsor that I was hurt and I needed to go home and recover for the spring swing, I was peering out my Motel 6 room window looking for a sign. I didn't see one, but I heard three!

As I pondered between competing and licking my wounds back home, I heard rounds of gunfire ring out. Being a lover and not a fighter, I made my decision to make the difficult call and disclose my injury along with my plan of returning for the last 10 stops of the year in the spring. My sponsor, if nothing else, was direct. He informed me that his business was not going well and that he could no longer sponsor me since I wasn't in the black for the fall swing. I informed him that I had three grand left and that he was welcome to it and apologized for any monies lost on my behalf. He appreciated the gesture but told me to keep it to pay my bills till I found a job or another sponsor.

~ *One More Time with Feeling* ~

I went home and rehabbed to take one last shot at the tour in Dallas. I had 3 months to get as ready as possible. I trained 3 hours a day. I went from 202 pounds to 171. I was in the best shape of my life for that stop. I had gained an equipment sponsorship from the biggest name in bowling, Brunswick.

I showed up nervous, but hopeful. This was my last shot, this was it. All my friends knew that my career hinged on this round of qualifying. I was right at the cutline all day long. Then as the final game came to an end, I needed to strike to stay alive and advance to the casher's round. My heart was pounding, my hands shook, but off my hand it was perfect.

I would leave a ten pin. I would miss cash by 8 points for eight games. My dream was over because of one pin per game. I went to my hotel and cried. It was brutal, but I made myself a promise to try one last time and win, lose or draw, I would accept the results. I went back and ran a pro shop for the guy that had put me out of business a couple years before. I was now divorced and bankrupt for a second time. Mom was right, I would fail multiple times.

I just went through the motions for a while. I still bowled some local stuff, just because I still loved competing. I stayed single, somehow. Not that I was a catch, but I am a serial relationship person. I jump from one to another. Hell, I married the first 2 people that I had sex with for Christ's sake. I broke that streak, thankfully, but I was not in a relationship in the traditional sense. I was at home on a Saturday afternoon, when there was a knock on the door. Nobody came to my house, ever.

Who in the world could it be? I opened my front door, and I couldn't believe who was standing on my front porch!

~ *47 Minutes* ~

It was Misty! I hadn't laid eyes on her in 3 years. She looked amazing! Even more beautiful than I remembered. It was an absolute blur. Just like it was in the beginning. I was so nervous. I cannot remember if I hugged her. I cannot remember what was said. The only thing that I can remember is just trying to breathe. My God, I still loved her as much as ever. I walked her to her car, and she leaned inside. I will admit that I checked her out. Man, I missed her! She pulled her child out of the car. She held her daughter and looked at me and smiled. She always wanted to be a mom. It suited her well. She looked happy, but why was she there then? We talked for a few and I asked how long she was in town and where she was staying, that much I remember. I watched her leave and walked back inside completely useless, and mind blown. I was supposed to go bowling that night, but that didn't happen. I called Misty instead.

She answered the phone at her mom's house. I asked her if I could come see her and take her out to get something to eat. She said yes and I told her what I always told her back in the days that I would pick her up for dates, I'll see you in 47 minutes. She laughed! I always loved her laugh!

So, 47 minutes later, I knocked on the door and was greeted by her mom. I got a hug and truly felt welcome. Misty was not quite ready. I think she was making me wait on purpose. When she did make her appearance, as usual, she was gorgeous! I walked her to my car and opened the door for her. It felt so good to open doors for her again. It felt good to see her again. It felt good just to be near her. I had missed her so much.

I took her to Denny's as she would not let me buy her a drink no matter what the establishment. We sat and talked for what felt like mere minutes, but hours had passed. She was married and had a small child. I didn't flirt and if I did it was involuntary. I just loved sitting across from her. It killed me not to hold her hand. I always held her hand. To the point that when we dated, I would shift the transmission with my left hand so that I wouldn't have to let go of her hand, even for a moment. I restrained every urge that I had out of respect for her and her family. We crossed no lines, not even close. I just gazed at her, remembering what used to be and wanting to have that back again. We left and I put her back in my car and we headed back to her mom's house.

As I drove those back roads that I had driven with her so many times, I hated that it was coming to an end. I felt as if my heart broke more and more as we edged closer and closer to her mom's house. Most of the night was a blur, but I vividly remember a couple things. As we approached the driveway, I told her something. I told her that if she ever ended up single again, to find me. I begged her to find me and that I would be hers, forever. She smiled and told me that I would have moved on and would probably have kids of my own. She said that she knew that I would be a good dad, and I would never break up my family for her. I walked her to the front porch like I had countless times before. I wanted to kiss her. She looked at me with a gaze that screamed that she was wondering if I was going to kiss her one more time. Out of respect for her, I didn't. I gave her a hug and whispered in her ear, "I've never stopped loving you." I felt her body get weak in my arms. She still loved me too, but she just couldn't say it. I turned around and looked over my shoulder and said only two more words, "find me." I got in my car; tears streaming down my face and drove 47 minutes home. I let her go, because I loved her. This would be the last time that I would hear her voice or see her face for nearly 20 years.

~ Going Blind ~

Once again, I was going through the motions. I was bowling in a league on a Wednesday night when my friend told me that he had someone that I should meet. My immediate response was nope! He pestered me for all 3 hours of league. Nope. Nope. Nope. Little did I know his wife was working on the other half of this blind date at the same time. Her reply, nope. Nope. Nope. I was sweaty. I was wearing torn blue jeans, a T-shirt and a baseball cap. I relented and so did she.

My friend went with me as his wife was with her. We arrived before the ladies, so we went to the bar at Henry Hudson's. I ordered a Zima or something else that was not manly. She approached and I was shocked that she wasn't homely. I said, "you can't be Allie." She asked why, and I said, "because you are beautiful." She grinned and I offered to buy her a drink. She said, jack and coke, I ordered two from the bartender as he delivered my Zima that I slyly slid over to my friend Stephen. Yes, our relationship started with a lie.

The basis for this was my own insecurity. Her ex was a civil servant, a fireman. He was a tremendous douchebag, but he ran toward danger, and I am not that dude. So, I pretended to drink hard liquor in hopes that I wouldn't seem like too much of a girly man. It was awkward and I was nervous. I was saying stupid stuff just to fill the gaps in conversation. I asked what she drove for Christ's sake, who the fuck does that? I am not shallow. Never have been, but it popped in my head and out it came. After 2 drinks, I offered to walk her to her car. I cut it short, later she would tell me that she wanted to stay with me longer. I asked her if I could take her on an actual date on Friday afternoon, she accepted with a grin. I liked her. Afterall, I married a blonde and a brunette, maybe this redhead was the answer.

I arrived for our first date, flowers in hand. Her door was open, and she was on her couch tying her shoes. She was very attractive. She was also taken aback by the fact that I bought her flowers. We set out on our date, and I opened her car door, when I got into the car she said, "you don't have to do that." I explained that it was just something that I was taught to do, and she'd have to get used to it. I was going to take her to the movies and then dinner. She rebuffed my plans and asked if I would take her to the zoo, I obliged.

After the zoo, it was time to get dinner. I told her she could pick any restaurant. She asked if I liked sushi. I said yes! Yet another lie. I wanted her to like me so badly. It wasn't long until she figured out that I had lied. There is just something about raw tuna. I bit into that and evidently, I turned green and nearly vomited. She told me that I could spit it out into my napkin as she laughed. I was busted, but it was funny. The date ended with a kiss on her doorstep, a kiss that could have easily led to more, but she sent me on my way. It seemed like she liked me, but I wasn't completely sure.

~ *On My Way* ~

I was hanging out at my house the next evening with a friend of mine and the phone rang. It was Allie. She asked if I wanted to meet her and her friends at a bar in Oklahoma City. I told her that I was on my way. I know it made me look eager, but I didn't care.

We talked and laughed at the bar until it was almost closed. She told me that she liked me so much that she didn't shave her legs so she wouldn't have sex with me on our second date. We walked across the parking lot to the hotel and each couple got a room. We were all talking in one room when she pulled me in and whispered in my ear, "I like spankings."

I picked her up out of the chair, looked at the other couple and said, "goodnight!" I carried her down the sidewalk to our room. Suddenly she didn't care if her legs were shaved. We didn't make love. We didn't even know each other. We had sex. After 20 minutes, she said, "you don't have to run the whole mile the first time." I was taken aback, shocked really. I finished and she took a shower. When she got out, her phone rang, it was her ex. He owned a bar, and he was closing it up. She told him that she was with me at a hotel, and he hung up on her. She looked at me and said, "don't you think it is weird that he called me after we had sex." I said, "no, he owns a bar, and we just shut one down." She wasn't over him and I knew it.

~ Bar Hopping ~

We went out a lot. I had never dated like that before. We danced and laughed. She would fill the gaps in conversation. She would ask me why I liked her so much. I would tell her that I always felt like I was the one who had to do all the talking, all the entertainment, but with her it was different. She entertained me. She made me laugh. She was beautiful and I had no intention of letting her slip through my fingers.

I became a daily fixture in her life. I just kept showing up. This infuriated her ex to no end. I could tell that she liked me. Even though she would tell me that she didn't. No really, we were driving down the street and she said, "you know that I don't even really like you that much." For some reason, I didn't believe her, and I just tried harder. I once sat on a couch with her, and she asked what I would change about her, and I said there was nothing. I asked the same question; she referenced that we weren't sexually compatible. Still, I kept trying harder. Then it happened.

~ Add Water Make Baby ~

Here's the deal. After my first marriage, I heard a rumor that Misty had stopped taking birth control from a friend of hers. Yet, we didn't conceive. My second wife went off birth control for nearly a year, yet no conception. Allie tried with her first husband, for years, yet never conceived. Allie and I were together for 2 months and she got pregnant. I honestly didn't think that I could have children. I always chalked it up to having chicken pox at 19 years old. I was shocked, but excited. She was astonished that I was happy and that I didn't run. I told my father, and naturally he wanted to meet her. So, my father, his wife and my grandmother met us at Zio's to have lunch. My father hugged her when he met her. He said, "I am so excited to meet my son's future wife!" He was smiling ear to ear when she replied, "oh just because I'm having his child doesn't mean I want to marry him." His smile vanished and I was crushed. It was not meant to be, she miscarried quickly.

She pushed me away, but I latched on harder. I just knew that I could show her enough love to win hers, I just knew it. We kept dating and she asked me what my five-year plan was. Yes, she asked me about my five-year plan. So, I, being twice divorced, twice bankrupt and working at a bowling alley for 9 bucks an hour told her my plan. I was planning on going to college to prove that I was intelligent and not just someone that could throw a bowling ball really well. She looked at me in disbelief. In a questioning tone she asked, "you're smart?" I replied, "I'm sure of it." I planned to major in Forensic Science. She got pregnant again and I enrolled immediately.

~ *A Matter of Motivation* ~

I went to college for a few weeks when I was 19. It wasn't "my money" perse, I had bowling scholarships. I was cocky when I went to college at the age of 19. I had never studied in high school; I didn't have to study. I went in with the wrong mentality the first time. I enrolled late, if you know anything about college, you know that the easy classes fill up early. The only biology class that had an opening was zoology. I took it. I'll never forget that professor.

He walked in and started speaking in a hauntingly intimidating voice. He said, I see we have some philosophy majors, accounting majors, English majors and some political science majors in this class this morning. I was an accounting major at 19. He said, my class isn't for you. You will not survive it. This class is for science majors, pre-med and the like. No shame in walking out now. I was offended. I stayed.

I perused the material for the first exam. I felt confident until I took the exam. He passed them out in order of grade once he was done with his onslaught of red ink. Top to bottom as he said. I waited a long time for my name to be called. I was out of my element. I dropped out of college after 3 weeks when I was 19. It didn't matter to me. I just wanted to bowl anyway.

Fast forward to the age of 27 and having a baby on the way. I once again made a last-minute decision to enroll in college. The same college as before. Forensic science was my major of choice now. I had all but blocked out my first debacle of 19-year-old me being caught on the chin in that zoology class.

I sat down in my first science class. I thought was ready, then my heart sank.

A familiar voice started rambling. I see we have some political science majors and some business majors in this classroom this morning. This class is not for you. You will not survive it and there is no shame in leaving now. It was the same motherfucker that cleaned my academic clock 8 years earlier. I was once again intimidated. I now had so much riding on me. It wasn't just about me anymore.

Here's the thing. Your motivation matters and Dr. Baird, that was his name, said it best. Fear is a great motivator. The clock was ticking. A baby on the way and no more plan B, there was only plan A. I knew the fallback of bowling was not an option. The money was so bad in bowling at that point, that some of the best in the world were living out of their cars just so they could keep competing. The only option was to get through this course.

~ Composition ~

I studied, really studied, because for the first time in my life it really mattered. I got an A in his course and every other course that I took that semester. I wasn't smarter than I was when I was 19, just more driven. I wanted to become something that Allie could be proud of, something that my kid would be proud of, hell something that I could be proud of as well.

I remember taking English composition. The roll was taken and when the Professor got to my name she paused. She asked my sister's name. I told her, she told me that my sister was the best writer she had ever had in her class and told me that I had quite a bit to live up to, to get out of her shadow. I quipped back and said, well she's adopted so don't get your hopes up too high. She laughed and I grinned. I told my sister about the exchange, as I thought she would get a kick out of it, which she did.

The semester flew by quickly. I was busy working, going to school and anxiously awaiting the arrival of our first child. Before I knew it, I was sitting in English Composition waiting for my final paper to be handed back to me. My professor failed to hand my final paper back to me but instead asked me to stay after class to talk with her. I obliged nervously. She asked if I recalled what she had said about my sister. I nodded in affirmation. She asked me to promise her something. She made me promise to write something. I was confused. I asked her what she meant. She said that I was now the best writer that she had ever taught and made me promise to write something one day. I explained that I had nothing to write about. She smiled softly and said, "I believe in my heart that one day you will because, you, young man, are a writer." I promised and left with my A and at my first opportunity I told my sister that she was no longer the best writer in the family while laughing the way that only little brothers can laugh. If you are reading this...promise kept Dr. Mayfield...promise kept.

~ *Your Baby is Gonna Starve* ~

I worked odd jobs during my first couple years of college. I was a telemarketer, I delivered pizza, I worked at a gas station and sold cars. Whatever I could find to put food on the table while starting my educational journey and preparing for the adventures of impending parenthood. Allie was adorable when she was pregnant. I loved it. I loved her. She would wake me up at 2 in the morning and say, "I want pancakes!" I would get dressed and we would go to IHOP, then I would go to class at 8am. I couldn't ever tell her no. I was so excited to have a family, and she was giving me that gift. Then our baby arrived! She was in labor for 20 hours. She was exhausted and so was I. I cried like a baby. I was so happy! I had no idea that I could love something so much. I was a daddy, and I loved it.

My mother-in-law showed up with Slim-Fast on the day of our daughter's birth. She told Allie that she had better lose weight or I would leave her because she was too fat. I threw her out of the room. Allie burst into tears. It wouldn't have mattered what she weighed. She was beautiful and I loved her dearly. My mother-in-law would never care much for me after that day, but that was fine with me. She hurt the woman I loved on the best day of our lives and to me, that was unforgivable. I had never seen a more beautiful sight than her holding our baby girl that day.

I went to work about a week later and got back into my routine. A fellow salesman asked what my major was, and I told him forensic science. He explained that his girlfriend had a master's degree in forensic science. Excited to get the scoop on the of life that lay ahead of me in forensic science, I asked where she worked. His reply floored me. She worked at Paper Warehouse because she couldn't find work. I panicked. What in the world was I going to do? I was only planning on getting a bachelor's degree. Then fate stepped in.

I was selling a car to a single mom, and I began arguing with the new car sales manager. I explained that she was a single mom and that I knew we could sell the car cheaper. My manager said and I quote, "Stoney Pride you are a shitty salesman. Your baby is gonna starve, your wife is gonna starve and you are gonna starve. All of you are gonna starve to death." He asked if I was good at math and science. I told him yes. He asked my major and I explained that I was currently trying to figure that out. He told me that he was a retired pharmacist and that I needed to investigate that because I cared too much about people to feed my child in any commissioned based line of work. I went home and researched.

~ *All Our Eggs* ~

I sat down and researched the prerequisites for pharmacy college. I had been in college for 18 months at this point. Every single course that I had taken since enrolling coincided with prepharmacy requisites. Every. Single. One. There was an application process and at that time only 1 in 10 applicants were accepted. I told Allie about the idea and asked if she was up for me being in school for an additional 3 years than we had planned in comparison to my original major. I explained it was more money for us later. She asked how much, about 80k more a year, 120K vs 40K. She asked if I thought that I could make the grades necessary to be accepted, if I thought that I could hack it in pharmacy college. I told her that I would make it happen for our family. She said, "then get it done babe!"

The courses got harder and harder. Advanced chemistry and calculus. I never had to study in high school. I studied constantly. I over studied. I was terrified of letting them down. My days were long, but she believed in me and put all her eggs in my basket and stayed home with Serenity. Speaking of eggs, going into my final year of prerequisites, we got pregnant again.

I was studying and loved the idea of having another child. All was well. I went to our 5-month OB appointment with her, having Serenity in tow. Serenity was normally a very happy baby, but she was inconsolable. Allie had me take her out to the car and wait for her to be finished. I did so. I was waiting at the curb for her. I could tell from her stride that something was very wrong.

She was in hysterics. We lost the baby. We cried in each other's arms. It was horrible. She'd have to have surgery; she'd have to have a D&C. I took the morning off from my organic chemistry class to be there for her. The surgery was only supposed to be 45 minutes long. I was bouncing Serenity on my knee while trying to study organic chemistry. An hour went by, nothing. An hour and a half went by, nothing. Then the hallway door flung open, and I saw the surgeon ripping off his gloves in anger while headed straight for me. I held Serenity tighter, thinking my God it's just her and I against the world now.

The surgeon sat down next to me and said, "everything went fine." I said, "really? That's how you walk out when things went well?" He explained that his mind was elsewhere. I told him that I thought I was a single parent for 30 seconds and he needs to control his shit a bit better if his wife was that big of a pain in the ass. We both laughed and I took Allie home.

There was a void between us, and we desperately wanted to fill it. Before we knew it, I was finishing my final semester of prepharmacy courses, and we were 7 months along with our son. It was Easter and suddenly Allie wasn't okay. I rushed her to the hospital. She had to have emergency gall bladder surgery. It was risky for her and our unborn son, but we had no choice.

The surgery went well, we wouldn't know until later the effects it would have on our son. For now, though, we pushed forward once more. As we entered her third trimester, I got invited for an interview at Southwestern Oklahoma State University's College of Pharmacy.

~ The Big "B" ~

The application process required me to submit a portfolio photo for my interview. This photo caused an argument between Allie and me. She had to take the photo. I walked into the living room of our duplex in a dress shirt and tie. She said, "nope, go put your Brunswick Pro Staffer shirt on for this photo." I said, "absolutely not. This is pharmacy. I just can't do it." She said, "it's who you are, you love it, you're putting on that shirt or I'm not taking your picture." I relented and complied. I just knew that it dashed my hopes of being accepted. Afterall, who has ever heard of a professional bowler turned pharmacist?

I was beside myself on the morning of my interview. I had only applied to one school. I couldn't afford to go anywhere else. I sat in the office and watched person after person complete their interview in 15 to 20 minutes. Then I got called back. I sat down at what seemed like the largest oak table in the world and waited for the first question. It was not what I was expecting. I was astonished.

Dr. Ramos was the professor that was interviewing me that morning. He was polite, soft spoken and well put together. I could almost feel myself sink in my chair as his gaze seemed transfixed on my portfolio photo. "Is that a Brunswick Pro Staff bowling shirt?' I grinned nervously and said yessir. He asked if I ever bowled against the number one ranked player in the world, Walter Ray Williams Jr. I told him my match play record against him was 1-1 with my loss being by one pin. Dr. Ramos was giddy with excitement. He explained that he grew up in a bowling alley that his best friend's family owned, and he loved bowling! We talked bowling for 45 minutes. My interview went well over an hour. I was in, not officially but I was in. I walked out to face a line of candidates looking worried and confused by the amount of time that had transpired since I disappeared into the interview area. I looked at them, shook my head in fabricated exhaustion and said, "good luck guys that was brutal!' They looked mortified and I walked to my car giggling. Yes, I can be a bit of a jerk.

~ Firsts and Lasts ~

I passed my finals to finish up my prerequisites for pharmacy school. We had one car, and Allie had taken Serenity to the doctor. We had no phone at all. I left her a note to tell her that I was walking a couple miles to go sell plasma to buy Serenity diapers and milk, promising that we wouldn't always be this broke, that it wouldn't always be this hard. I felt like a failure. It couldn't get much worse. Could it?

Then on a Friday night, gunshots rang out outside of our duplex in Norman. I ran to Serenity's crib and pulled her out and laid my body across hers to shield her from bullets that could rip through our walls. I remember Serenity crying and looking at Allie. I told her that we'd never be in this bad of a place again. I had not received my acceptance letter yet, but I moved us from Norman to Weatherford anyway. I told my classmates what had happened and that I was moving our family without being accepted yet. My friend Donnie shook his head in with a combination of disbelief and admiration. I told him, "Sometimes you just got to act like things are going to work out." Within a week of our arrival, I got accepted to pharmacy school. Now, I had a real chance to give us a better life!

I had the summer off from school, the only break that I ever had since starting my college journey. It was during this time that we had our son. He was a little early and had jaundice. I laid on the floor with him for a week when they sent us home with a Billi light. He was strong and healthy, especially his lungs! Serenity was quiet, Stoney was a crier, just as I was when I was a baby. He would be our last, we even joked later, that even if he was our first, he would still have been our last. Serenity instantly wanted to mother and smother him with love. She adored her bubba from the moment she laid eyes on him.

I loved my first semester of pharmacy school. No more bullshit courses. Every single course mattered. Every course meant something for my career. No more humanities professors acting like they were curing cancer. It was tough, but it was an awesome feeling. For the first time, I truly felt that I belonged somewhere that had nothing to do with throwing a bowling ball. I excelled in all my classes. With each exam that I passed, I felt more and more sure that I truly deserved to be there. I could see the finish line. I could see a better life for us and our little family. I finished the semester with all A's, I even got an A in lab, which usually eluded me in my undergrad coursework. What could stop me now?

~ *The Fork* ~

As I entered my second semester, I was more hopeful than ever. My daily schedule was insane, but I loved it. My days had been blending together for quite some time. My days would start around 4:30 in the morning, when I would study until I would head to class at 8 am. I would then be in class until 4 or 5pm. I would then spend time with my wife and kids until 8pm, then I would study and burn the candle from the other end until midnight. I would then collapse into bed and start all over again bright and early with just a few hours of sleep. It was worth it to me. I was getting an education, and I was getting to spend time with my wife and kids. I was tired, but I was happy. I felt worthy of my spot at Southwestern

Oklahoma State. I excelled in every course. I felt like I belonged. I felt like everything was finally going to work out in our favor. Until one morning, I felt something else.

I woke up not to a screaming alarm clock, but instead to screaming back pain. As I was ripped into consciousness, I yelped and writhed back and forth in bed. It was 3 in the morning. I couldn't stand the thought of having the kids and her in the hospital waiting room during flu season, so I opted to take myself to the local emergency room. The hospital was only a mile or so away from our little house. As I drove there, I heard echoes of every cautionary tale about getting sick in that town. The hospital had quite the reputation in terms of the quality of care that one could hope to receive in that old brick one story building that looked more like an old nursing home than a fully functioning hospital.   However, any echoes were soon drowned out by the searing pain of the worst muscle spasms that I had ever experienced in my life. It felt as if someone had a fork in between my shoulder blades and the tines of the fork were twisting the muscle fibers in my back. Turns out that the perceived fork was not the only twist headed my way.

~ They're Busy with Other Patients ~

The waiting room was nearly empty, and I was in a room in what seemed like mere minutes.   As I waited to see the doctor, which would later turn out to be a physician's assistant, my hands and feet were starting to tingle. I looked around the exam room. The paint was peeling from the walls, ceiling tiles were stained and I just kept remembering watching One Flew Over the Cuckoo's nest as a child...this was eerily similar.

I was still writhing in pain and describing it as best I could. I was discounted. In fact, I was treated like a drug seeker. I saw the looks. I heard the tones. I knew what they thought. I waited and waited. The clock was ticking, I thought only in terms of making it to my first class on time, but in reality it was ticking in a much more dire way.

It pissed me off. The physician's assistant gave me a quick once over and said it was just a pinched nerve. By this time my hands and my feet tingled even more, and the back pain was worsening by the minute. The PA insisted that it was a pinched nerve and said that she didn't normally write for muscle relaxers but would make an exception. I told her that I didn't want pain meds. I just wanted to know why my back hurt and my hands and feet felt funny. I told her it didn't make sense and asked to see the doctor. I was told that the doctor was busy with other patients. I was offended, I refused the pain medication each time they entered the room, and they had offered it to me. The last time I refused the med; I outright told them that I didn't want pain medication. They discharged me with a script for Soma and told me to go home and go to sleep. I had to be in class in an hour, so that wasn't happening.

~ *Fading* ~

I rushed home, changed clothes and walked to school. It was January 25th, 2007, and it was now snowing. I walked to school on most of the days of the week. The rage of an ER dismissal of my condition fueled my steps to class. I left my script for muscle relaxers at the house for Allie to drop off at the pharmacy for me. I left the van at the house for Allie and the kiddos, as it was my longest school day of the week and wouldn't get out of class until 5pm. It was only about a mile walk to campus and as usual I fumbled through note cards studying on my journey to my first class of the day,

Pathophysiology II. The professor was Dr. Ramos, the very man that interviewed me for my admission to the program.

It was my favorite course; Dr. Ramos had a passion for his profession. I was a bit more tired than my usual level of exhaustion but attributed it to my early morning adventure at the local emergency room. The muscle spasm was still there, but by the end of the class it was growing more faint by the moment, perhaps it was just a muscle spasm. Perhaps, I was just paranoid.

Dr. Ramos was the kind of professor that everybody loved. He was genuine and you could tell that he enjoyed what he did. Today we were covering the musculoskeletal system.   Some of my classmates seemed detached from the lecture, but I wasn't. I was the last class to enter the program without Anatomy and Physiology being a prerequisite to apply.   Most students applied to other universities which already required A&P, so for them some of this was review, but it was all new to me so I soaked up as much as I could in order to play catch up with my peers. Specifically, that day we covered the gastrointestinal tract, and the different types of muscles involved in the process of digestion, from the mouth to the eventual delivery to the toilet and everything in between. By the end of class, my back no longer hurt at all, but man I was tired. Luckily my next class was just 2 doors down the hall.

~ *Reassurance of a Mentor* ~

I made it to class and plopped down in my chair, I remember getting an odd look from one of my friends and he asked if I was alright in a half joking manner. After all I hit my chair as if I had been hitting the sauce all night. I just repeated what I had been feeling, "I am just so damn tired!" I barely remember the class at all, if it hadn't required me to work out pharmacokinetics problems, I would have fallen asleep at my desk. Class was over before I knew it and it was lunch time; I skipped lunch and instead I headed to see Dr. Ramos in his office.

There was only one elevator in the building. I was at the other end of hall that seemed to stretch farther and farther each time that I glanced down it. On the other hand, I was right next to the stairs. I opted to traverse two flights of stairs to meet with my favorite professor, hell he was my mentor. It felt like it was twenty flights instead of two, I was exhausted, and my legs felt a little heavy, but I managed to get to his office. I knocked on his door and went in to talk to him like I had so many times before, except this time I was asking not about class content, but about myself. We got along because we were both 'how' guys, not 'what' guys. We knew that understanding the how made the what so much easier to remember. Today however, I showed up with a what question. I explained my early morning wake-up call ala back spasm and my sudden onset of increased fatigue. He asked me to walk him through my usual day. I explained my early morning studying, days filled with classes and studies, dinner and playtime with my babies and wife, then studying after they went to bed until about midnight and then starting all over again each morning. He shook his head and told me that he really thought that I was doing more than I should and that I needed some rest. I remember him saying the windedness was a little odd, but I needed to rest up this coming weekend seeing as how it was Thursday, and he bet I would feel better come Monday. I truly enjoyed our talks, he had the ability to be a mentor, a friend and a psychologist all at once. I agreed with his assessment and shuffled down the hall to lab for the final four hours of my school day.

~ Annoyance, Disobedience and the Walk ~

Lab was annoying. I was never really a fan of labs, but that day it was nothing less than fucking annoying. I wasn't sure why it was so annoying, but it sure was fucking annoying. I remember using balances to measure powders with wax paper. I was so tired by this point that I was fumbling the powder, I was having to concentrate harder and harder on getting my hands to obey. It was taking me longer than usual to do my work. I was skipping steps, using poor technique and was having to be corrected by my professor, which was a first for me which left me even further annoyed. I was so mad that I was seething, it was out of character for me, to the point that my friend Donnie said, "dude it is okay." That centered me a bit as I usually had a pretty good handle on my emotions. Soon, it was time to start walking home. I was ready for that, or so I thought.

My journey home usually took me about 20 minutes by foot. This time it took me longer, much longer. My legs seemed heavier by the minute. I was winded before I started. I did not have a cell phone we couldn't afford more than one and Allie and the kiddos took priority in terms of communication needs. So, there was no lifeline, just the occasional car that passed me by on the side streets between the school and my house. Twenty minutes passed and I wasn't even halfway home, I staggered in exhaustion, my mind still chalking it up to a lack of sleep, but my heart knowing that it wasn't. It was now completely dark, but I could see the light shining in our utility room from a block away, I made it to our front porch about an hour after starting my seemingly drunken stagger home from school. I just stood and stared at those 3 steps on my porch. They now made the two flights that I had taken to get to Dr Ramos' office earlier seem like a walk in the park. Something wasn't right, but I couldn't figure it out. However, a clue awaited me at the kitchen table.

~ The Clue in the Kitchen ~

I had to use my arms to pull my legs upward on each step. It felt like it took 10 minutes to go up the three steps to reach our front porch. I forced my way up and into the safe harbor of our living room, something smelled good.

Allie was in the kitchen and had expected me to be home a little sooner, but she had dinner ready, and it was my favorite, chicken fried steak. She took one look at me and immediately asked if I was alright. Again, I simply stated that, "I am just so damn tired." She pointed to my chair at the table and said, "sit down and eat something baby." I obliged and shuffled my way to my chair. She had gone to so much trouble and it looked perfect; I was ready for something to go right for me that day. I grabbed my knife and fork and cut a piece of chicken fried steak and chewed it up, even that was tiring. I swallowed it, yet I didn't. It tried to go down my trachea instead of my esophagus. I gagged and coughed it up and spit it into my napkin. I remember her giving me a very confused look. I played it off and said out loud, "slow down fat boy!" She giggled and so did I. I cut a second piece, smaller this time, and chewed it up, thoroughly. I swallowed it, and again I gagged. This time there was no joking, no shrugging it off as eating too fast, this time I knew. I knew something was wrong and for some reason, God had prepared me for this moment. Every right decision, every wrong decision, every triumph and every failure had literally put me in the seat that I needed to be earlier that morning and by doing so, what was happening at that kitchen table was pulled together enough to give me a clue.

~ The Wrong Pipe? ~

I was confused, until that moment. I still didn't know everything that I needed to know, but I knew enough. I knew enough. I looked at Allie and as soon as I stopped coughing and gagging, I said only 4 words, "we gotta go now!"

You see that morning when I was seen in the emergency room and was told to go home and take a muscle relaxer and get rest, well I didn't listen. I rarely do. I went ahead and went to class. I went to my favorite class. The class that teaches the 'how' and 'why' of the human body, Pathophysiology II. It was that very morning that I learned about the structure of the muscles of the human body, more specifically and most importantly, I knew it now, I learned about the upper esophageal sphincter. It is the muscle that controls the passage of food and water at the top of the esophagus. It allows us to keep food and water from being aspirated into our lungs when we eat and drink. I learned that it was voluntary skeletal muscle that very morning. So, the second time that I gagged on my chicken fried steak, that's when it hit me. The exhaustion from moving my body, my legs being so sluggish, me fumbling the weighing papers in lab and now trouble swallowing. I did not know what was wrong, but I knew that everything that was wrong so far involved voluntary skeletal muscle and that told me that I needed to get to a hospital. Allie agreed with my ramblings and asked if I could change little Stoney's diaper while she got Serenity ready, I nodded and made my way to my son who was lying on a blanket on the floor and kneeled over his fragile body and my 250-pound frame lost its balance and I crashed to the floor!

~ Mixed Signals ~

Somehow, I managed to straddle his body and catch myself with a tremendous thud on the ceramic tile floor. Allie heard the noise and rushed into the living room. It scared me so badly that I was shaking. She rushed to the hallway door and asked if I was okay to change him and handed me the box of wipes. I said yes and reached into the box of wipes and screamed in agony. I shoved the box away from me and checked my hand for burns and blisters. The wipes burned me so badly, yet there was no blister. To me, they were scalding hot, yet to anyone else on the planet, they were cool to the touch, what the hell was going on?

We got loaded in the van. Allie didn't even ask if we were going back to the local hospital, she just flew past it and got on the highway headed toward Oklahoma City. She was driving that Ford Focus as fast as she could. I was hardly ever sick at all, but she knew something was up, we both did. We got to Yukon and pulled into the hospital parking lot. I was weaker but still staggered into the emergency room waiting area. Allie with little Stoney in a car-seat and Serenity holding her hand, started getting me checked in and within minutes I was getting vitals taken and blood was being drawn.

Soon doctors were asking questions about my current state and were in and out the room several times. Then they returned with a couple doctors at once and started a neurological examination. One doctor had me touch my index finger to my nose and then instructed me to touch my fingertip to his fingertip while he held it out in front of me. I missed the tip of my nose slightly but missed his fingertip by at least a foot. He checked my patellar reflexes, you know, the little hammer on the knee. My leg jerked as it should. The doctors shot looks around the room at each other and at us. He then asked if I could stand up.

It took a bit more of my strength, but I did stand up unassisted. One doctor got behind me and the other doctor stood in front of me. I was told to stretch my arms out to make a cross shape with my body, close my eyes and see if I could keep my balance. I was told not to worry about falling as the doctor behind me would catch me if I should become unsteady. I closed my eyes.

~ *Not the Usual Patient* ~

I didn't feel anything, until I was caught by the doctor at a 45-degree angle. I was falling and my mind and body were not even processing it! They helped me to the table and stepped out for a moment. Allie looked more worried, as I am sure that I did as well. The air in that room became heavier, dense with worry. Allie kissed me goodbye and took our kids over to my sister's house that was just a few miles away, as they were restless, and it looked like I was going to be there for a while. She called my sister and let her know what was going on and left for her house. My brother-in-law, Chris, showed up in what seemed to be mere moments after the call. He was there when the doctors came back in with information about what was happening to me.

They led with a question, as doctors sometimes do. "You are a studying to be a pharmacist, right?" I nodded in agreement. "Well, I am going to tell you more than I would a usual patient. Because of your knowledge base." Now let's think about that for just a moment. A byproduct of my education in progress, somehow this makes me stronger emotionally. Somehow it makes me less human. Less scared? Anyhow, they then proceeded to tell me that I was going to be transferred to Baptist Medical Center in Oklahoma City as they were much better equipped to provide me care going forward. His actual words were, "we can't save you here, but they can at Baptist." They then told me that my differential diagnosis was between multiple sclerosis and Guillain Barre Syndrome. They then asked if I understood the gravity of those possibilities. To which I answered, "come on Guillain Barre," in an audibly shaken voice. "I can beat that one, right? You don't beat MS, but I can beat Guillain Barre right?" I wanted some sort of assurance. One of the doctors said, "yeah you can beat that, but this is moving faster than anything that I have ever seen." They walked out of the room and then my brother-in-law asked about the prognosis of each. I lost it. Then it hit me. It hit me how stupid that I had been. I was 30 and I was invincible, or so I thought. I had a wife who had put her life on hold and put all her chips in a pile and bet on me to win for us. We had a 2-year-old daughter and a six-month-old son, facing potentially fatal outcomes and I had not one penny of life insurance. I grabbed Chris' shirt and begged him to promise that he would make sure that my wife and kids always had a place to stay. Tears streaming down my face, panicking not for myself, but for my family and their well-being. For the first time in my life, I understood my mother and how she was able to not give a damn about herself but instead fret and worry about all the variables that swirled around the ones that she loved so much. I once again began negotiating with God.

~ *No Stops Allowed* ~

I begged God to let me see my children grow up. I didn't care if I walked or if I was confined to a wheelchair forever. I simply wanted to see them reach 18 years old, I couldn't stand the thought of not being there for them if they needed me. I couldn't fathom a world where I didn't stand between my children and all the dangers that the world possesses, even if the 'standing' part was figurative. Allie walked back into the room as I was wrapping up negotiations with the almighty healer.

I updated Allie with the latest prognosis. She went quiet. I could see the wheels turning. I could see that the wreckage in my mind was obvious to her. It wasn't long before the doctor came back into the room with the nurse. I welcomed the interruption of our worried silence. I was fearful and it was honestly hard to say the things out loud that I needed to without me breaking down. Every time I thought of something to say, all that I could see was Serenity and Stoney growing up without me. I was jerked back to attention with what the doctor said next.

"We can't save you here. We aren't equipped for it." If that doesn't get your attention, I don't know what will. I was being transferred to Baptist Hospital. There was a lot of traumas in the area for some reason and I was still deemed non-critical at this point. It would be a while before an ambulance would be secured for my transport. The doctor looked at Allie and said that he would give us the option of self-transport if we promised not to make a single stop in between the two hospitals. We both looked at him a bit puzzled until he said, "because this is the last time you're going to be alone together for a long time." We took him up on his offer…

~ That's How Rare You Are ~

I was less coordinated than I was just an hour ago. The nurse wheeled me to the front door and Allie said she'd grab the van, I declined and said that I could walk to it. I stood up and started making my way to the van. Each step required more thought than the last. It was not technically far; it was in the first row of spaces. I was moving okay; but it felt as if my shoes were waterlogged. There was a curb, a strip of grass and a tree between me and the van. I stopped, stared at it and mustered the strength to raise my leg for the 8-inch climb.

I made it onto the grass, but when I took my second step I stumbled and had to catch myself. I wrapped my arms around the tree and clung to it as hard as I was clinging to what I thought of as reality just hours ago, a reality that would never exist again. I made it to the van, and she started driving. It was about a twenty-minute drive, there was silence for 15 minutes. My mind was racing. I couldn't take the silence any longer. "I am going to be okay. I promise." That was the best that I could come up with. Those were my words of comfort to the mother of my children. Her reply shook me to my core. "No, you're not. You are not going to be okay." Bewildered and at a loss for words, we sat in silence for the rest of way to the emergency room entrance at Baptist.

The emergency room was packed. It was January 25th after all, the height of flu season. We were met with a wheelchair, which I immediately collapsed into. There was no waiting room for me, no triage, I was wheeled straight passed a packed waiting room filled with people who had been waiting there for God only knows how long. They began checking my vitals as usual and told me that Dr. Lawrence, chief neurologist, was making his way to the hospital. It was now approaching 10pm. The nurse said that the neurologist had not been to the hospital after 6pm in 15 years. She said that is how rare you are sir. In what seemed like mere moments later, he entered the room, and I was taken aback by what I saw.

~ *No Room for Bullshit in Leather Satchels* ~

As if the day wasn't surreal enough, Dr Lawrence made his way into my room. It was as if he was a character in a movie. It was as if he stepped out of a DeLorean equipped with a flux capacitor, 1.21 gigawatts and all. His clothes were classic in nature. No scrubs. No tennis shoes. Thin laced dress shoes, dress slacks, a tie, a button-down vest, glasses with a spare set hanging out of his pocket and a leather medical satchel, that in and of itself appeared to be the better part of 50 years old, likely one of the very first things he bought for himself to use in his profession. He was all business. He pulled no punches with what he was about to say to us.

"Patellar reflexes, did you have them in Yukon?" he asked. I answered yes. He checked my reflexes; they were now completely absent. He asked how long ago they had checked them; it was only about 45 minutes earlier. He did all the other neurological tests again. Then came the hard part. He started talking. "You're a pharmacy student, right?" He said, "I am not going to subject you to a spinal tap, you could already be in more pain than you can imagine soon. You are an open and shut case of Guillain Barre Syndrome. You are a slam dunk young man. You are going to lose the ability to walk, talk, eat, drink, probably won't be able to breathe on your own much longer and you are going to be in ICU for a long time. There is a chance that you could die from this; it is that serious. What questions do you have for me?"

I immediately shifted to pharmacist mode; I asked what the treatment of choice was to combat Guillain Barre. It was IVIG. I looked at the doctor and said, "let's get it started now, I've already got an IV going." He responded that it wasn't something that was just ready, that it had to be compounded. In the meantime, my room was ready in ICU. The doctor walked out and left Allie and I to ourselves. She looked shattered. She looked at me, her husband, the father of her children and I was crumbling more and more by the minute. There was no backup plan. I looked at her and said, "I swear to God I will not die on you." She replied, "You better not. Don't you dare leave me with our two babies." We had bet it all on me to win, to finish school, to provide for us. I was to be the hero of our story. I was Superman, but kryptonite was coursing through my veins. My arms now felt heavy as the nurses came to wheel me to ICU.

~ *The Name of the Game* ~

As I made my journey through corridors and elevators, I went through the checklist of things to come as I prepared to fight this thing called Guillain Barre. First, I would never really know how it was triggered. I had had the flu, a bleeding ulcer and was burning the candle at both ends. That was frustrating for me, but I had it now, for whatever reason, and now I had to focus. What I knew at this point was that it was my own immune system, I was my own worst enemy, literally. My immune system recognized my nerves as non-self, as a danger. It was destroying the insulation, the myelin sheath, that covers my nerves. The nerve impulses were no longer guided efficiently toward their destination. The impulse was being bled out more and more, which is why my arms and legs felt heavy. This would eventually cause paralysis, which was hard to wrap my mind around as I could still move. Guillain Barre is defined by what is called ascending paralysis. Which means that it starts at your fingers and toes and then works its way toward the center of your body. That is where the main threat lies, the diaphragm. If it makes it there, I would have to be put on a ventilator. I had just studied about the seriousness of ventilator pneumonia. That was the foe that scared me. That was the one that could end me, and I knew it. I was snapped back to reality when the nurse said, "Stoney Pride, ICU bed 7." I had arrived in my new home. This is where my fight would start.

They wheeled my transport bed next to my ICU bed. They had eight people in the room with me, each grabbed my sheet and prepared to move me to my new bed, I told them no! They stopped and looked at me confused. They asked if I was hurting, I said no. They asked what was wrong? I told them, "Nothing's wrong, I can still move myself over and want to do it while I still can." They shot looks at each other and allowed me to try. I moved myself; it was harder than I let on, but they nodded with equal parts of surprise and hopefulness. I settled in and waited for what was to come. Within a few minutes someone in the ICU coded.   That sent shockwaves through me. It signified the seriousness of where I now resided. The respiratory therapist rolled in and said, "we need to get a baseline assessment of your lung capacity." This was the name of the game, and I was about to see what sort of cards I had been dealt. I performed the test and waited for the bad news to start rolling in, the therapist looked at me in disbelief.

~ Liters and Laps ~

The average human has a lung capacity between 4 and 6 liters. The reason for the shocked expression on the therapist's face? My lung capacity was 7.6 liters! The lungs of an athlete resided within the chest wall of an obese 30-year-old man that had not worked out consistently in 3 years. The therapist looked at me and said, "you have no idea how lucky you are to start at 7.6 liters. That's awesome!" I still had my sense of humor intact, so I said, "well I've been awesome all my life, why stop now?" I'll never forget that she giggled as she walked to the door, turned back toward me and gave me the most forced grin I had ever seen and sighed. She knew what was coming, I could tell that she hated knowing what lay ahead of me.

I was getting a bit more uncomfortable, but it wasn't too bad. I had strict instructions that I was not allowed to move without having nurses present. I had to move. I was restless. I called the nurse. I asked the nurse if I could walk around, while I still had the ability to do so. They refused. I begged. They said that they would ask the doctor. They demeaned me by forcing me to use a walker, but I accepted the deal. I started walking around the ICU. I could hear the beeping monitors, the moans of the other patients, but most of all the sound of ventilators echoed in my head. I looked up and I had just walked a full lap around ICU. The nurse said, "okay, back to bed." I begged her to go again; she reluctantly allowed me to try to make it around again. I didn't make it around one more time, instead I did two more laps. I gained comfort from the hopeful looks of the staff. Their looks said that I might be alright. That comfort and those looks were to be short lived.

~ Hit the Button ~

When I climbed back into my bed, the IVIG had arrived, and they started the drip. There was a sense of relief that I had started treatment. Instead of only the problems coursing through my veins, the solution was now coursing through as well. I began cramping in my lower back and gut. So, like a good boy, I hit the nurse's call button and waited for permission to potty. The nurse asked if I felt okay to move the 2 feet to the toilet beside my bed. I, in a nearly offended tone said, "well yeah, I only hit the button because you said I had to do it." She held my arm for support, but I managed to get to the toilet and was left to handle my business. Nothing occurred. I hit the button again, she asked if I could get up, I nodded and pushed myself up using the bars around the toilet and triumphantly got back into bed. Within 30 minutes I was cramping again. I again hit the button, she again asked if I could get out of bed. I was still defiant and confident. I made it over with a bit more difficulty. When I finished, she came back in and said "OKAY, can you get back?" I nodded and pushed downward with my arms. I was mortified.

Where just 30 minutes ago, I had pushed myself to my feet, now my arms simply tremored and shook trying to push against the weight of my body. I shook my head in disbelief. I began tearing up. It was now real. It really was going to happen the way that they said that it would. Allie looked on in disbelief as to how quickly the strength had left me. Disbelief that something that we couldn't see was destroying her husband, the father of her children. The nurse consoled me and helped me to my feet, and I got back into bed. She placed a urinal and bedpan next to me and simply said, "I'm sorry" as my respiratory therapist made her way back into the room to check the speed of my demise in terms of my lung capacity.

~ Two ~

Two hours had passed since my lung volume was checked. I wasn't as confident as I had been. I performed the test; I felt no different. She wrote it down and said, "you're still in good shape, we are going to start checking you hourly." I didn't accept that answer. I was at 7.6 to start. I needed to know what the reading was now. I asked her, she replied, "it is now 5.8 you're okay, but it is falling." I was no longer an Olympian. I was now in the average human range. My least favorite medical professional entered the room shortly after the respiratory therapist left. I really didn't care for him.

As my humanity and dignity were being peeled away one layer at a time, the pulmonologist began to lay out his plans for my salvation. He was cold, calculating and completely detached. He explained the events that were racing toward me. He spoke of when my breathing would become labored, he spoke of the feeling of drowning on dry land. He gave me the number. The number that he would allow my lung volume to fall to before he would put me on a ventilator. That number without exception was 2.0. Under 2.0, it was no longer my fight. He left the room as coldly as he entered it. Allie and I looked at each other with a 'what the fuck' expression on our faces. I was exhausted, I looked at Allie and told her I was going to try to sleep. I had no idea what the situation would be when I woke up, it's a good thing that I didn't, or I would not have fallen asleep.

~ *30 Minutes* ~

I woke up 30 minutes later. I began cramping again, worse than ever. I looked at the bedpan and I wasn't ready for that. I hit the nurse's button. The nurse came in and asked what I needed. I said I needed to get to the toilet. She reiterated that I needed to use the bedpan. I looked at her with a mixture of sadness, defeat and anger. I begged her to let me try once more. She said, "can you make it there?" I nodded yes. She told me that only if I was sure that I could make it. I assured her that I could make it. She said, "alright Mr. Pride, go for it." I swung my arms, but my legs didn't budge. Thirty minutes ago, they moved. Now, I was paralyzed from the waist down. Allie ran across the room to me. I looked toward the nurse frantically. I said, "thirty minutes, that's all it took? That's all it took to completely lose my legs?" The nurse tried to hide her concern, but I could see it. Not too long ago, an hour or two I was walking around the ICU. She assured us that I was exactly where I needed to be. She walked out and moments later in walked respiratory therapy, this guy was new. How far had I fallen now?

My arms were a bit heavier, but I could still grasp the mask to do my breathing test. I gave it all that I had in me. I anxiously asked for the new result. It had fallen to 5.0. Clinging to my sense of humor, to which I replied, "rag top down so my hair can blow." He looked up with a grin and said, "girlies on standby, waiting just to say hi. Did you stop?" Then we both said, "no I just rolled by." We both laughed hysterically. He patted me on the arm and said, "keep that sense of humor bro." It felt so good to laugh for a moment. To forget for just a few seconds the gravity of the situation that I was in that night. Before I could consider falling asleep the staff came in to discuss plans that scared me more than I already had been.

~ *Yogurt* ~

Now here's the thing about Guillain Barre Syndrome. It attacks the peripheral nervous system, it spares the central nervous system, physically the brain is unaffected. This leads to the aforementioned plan. It centered around setting up communication. I was hit with it. If I lost the ability to speak, we had to work out alternate communication. If I could still nod, yes and no questions would be easy. If I could still wiggle fingers, one wiggle would be yes, two was no. My toes were no longer an option as they were completely paralyzed. Then if I couldn't do the above any longer, one blink of the eyes was yes, two was no. Then I asked the question that I didn't want the answer to, "what if I can't do any of the above?" The doctor answered bluntly and honestly, "then you will be a prisoner in your own body, completely aware of everything going on around you and inside of you, but unable to communicate whatsoever perhaps for weeks or months." The last time I fell asleep I woke up paralyzed from the waist down. I was terrified of sleep now more than ever. I was terrified that I would wake up a prisoner in my own body.

Allie left and my brother-in-law took watch over me for the rest of the night. I fought sleep with everything I had in me. Somehow, I made it to morning, I made it to my second round of IVIG. I again was hopeful that it would kick in and start to slow the process. I got visited by the dietician and physical therapists. I was put on a soft, non-solid diet for fear of aspiration. They brought me yogurt to see if I could pass the test and not choke on it. My father walked in as they sat it in front of me. He was just in time to see what he didn't want to see.

I had not tried to grasp anything in hours. I tried to grab the spoon but couldn't. I tried with two hands, but I couldn't. I could see my father's heart break at that moment. In that moment it became real for him. In that moment, I realized that the IVIG was not slowing the disease process. My father fought back tears as he picked up my spoon and fed me yogurt like an infant. My father said perhaps the saddest, yet truest thing that he ever uttered. "Now I know why your mom died. If she had to see you like this, this would have killed her. You need your momma so badly son, but she never needed to see you like this." I agreed in silence and got the yogurt down okay.

I was taken by surprise by the next symptom that had emerged. I just sulked. He asked me what was wrong? I had no sense of taste whatsoever. In the grand scheme of what was going on, sure it was nothing. But there was a reason that I entered the ICU at 250 pounds, I loved food, and it showed. I had lost the use of my legs, I was in pain, I couldn't feed myself, but God damn it! Now I can't taste food. This was some bullshit. I was fully engaged in my pity party and looked up to see that the respiratory therapist was back. I said, "oh you're back to check on wheezy?" I wasn't ready to give up my sense of humor just yet. I also wasn't ready for what was about to happen next either.

~ Uuuuck ~

The respiratory therapist handed me the mask as usual. It was a larger object than the spoon, so I could still grasp it with both hands. I held it to my face and proceeded with the test. It came back with a result of 2.5 liters. My face was numb, my hands were weak. I panicked. I couldn't be that close to a ventilator. Not yet. I asked the therapist to hold the mask down on my face as I was losing strength and coordination. She obliged, and even with her assistance, my reading had dipped to 3.8. I lost half of my lung capacity in 12 hours. Except for a 30-minute nap, I had been awake for around 30 hours. I needed sleep, but was still terrified that I would wake up completely paralyzed. I began to drift off.

I would jerk awake within seconds or minutes throughout the day. There was not much rest to be had in ICU anyway. You can get better in the ICU, but you will never get well in ICU. The labs and monitoring are relentless, they must be. Afterall, they think that you are dying. Day 2 brought my newest symptom, drunk speech. I was now slurring as if I had done about 12 shots of tequila. It was funny to me at first. Then the unthinkable happened. I lost control of my lower lip. I could no longer drink with a straw, but that's not the worst part. I lost my ability to pronounce the 'f' sound. I could no longer say the word fuck. So, if you remember the flags being at half-mast on January 26, 2007, that's why. It was an ucking tragedy.

~ *Go Get Billy* ~

My lung volume numbers continued to dwindle throughout the day. By the end of day 2, I was all the way down to 2.1. I had a new demand for my respiratory therapist team. They looked at me like I was crazy. I wasn't crazy. It was what needed to be done. Had anyone else ever had this idea? I'm going to bet not, but in my mind, it made sense. Was it pleasant? No. Could it keep me safe for a little while longer? That's what I was betting on. So, I asked the question.

"Who is the biggest, strongest worker on this floor?" That was the question that I asked after the next check of my lung volume. That was my next question after she told me the reading had dropped to 2.1. She asked why. I told her that she might feel sorry for me, she might be afraid to hurt me, she might not get a good seal when she pressed the mask to my face when testing my lung volume. I could hardly hold the mask at all, I was down to gross, uncoordinated movements with my arms. I was panicking that I would be vented before I truly reached the <2.0 threshold. She replied, Billy. With slurred speech, I told her to go get him. I begged her not to put 2.1 in my chart. With tears streaming down my face, I begged her.

She relented and went to get Billy. He was like me. Only he wasn't sick. He was like I was just 3 days earlier. I saw how he looked at me. He hadn't ever been asked to do this before. I tried to put him at ease. I slurred, "this isn't my first time, you can be rough with me." He grinned and shook his head. He grabbed the back of my head and pressed the mask against my face. I could hardly feel it. I could see the effort. The reading 2.4. I had just bought myself some more time. I collapsed into my pillow and went limp. My doctors had a new plan for day 3.

~ Detox ~

I was tumbling faster and faster. The plan of confusing my immune system with IVIG wasn't working as intended. On the morning of day 3, I could feel the heaviness in my chest. I was no longer moving the air well enough on my own. Suddenly there were 7 medical staff in the room with me. They explained what they were about to do. They had shifted the strategy to plasmapheresis. It involved placing a line in my neck that led down to the top of my heart. I had become so unstable that the increase in population in my room was the crash team. The team that would bring me back if my heart stopped or if the vein in my neck blew out and I started bleeding uncontrollably. The nurse told me to bear down so she could gain access to the vein in the safest way possible. I didn't even know if I had the strength to do that any longer. I had no jokes left in me, only fear.

The line was placed without incident. Each treatment would take 4 hours. The purpose was akin to an oil change. It would entail 60% of my plasma being removed and replaced with donor/synthetic plasma each day. My body had developed antibodies that were destroying my nerves. Each treatment would be removing some of those antibodies. This would be done once daily with a plan of doing it for 5 days. There were risks and I was not allowed to be alone during the 4-hour procedure. It was day 3 and it was time for the first treatment.

The best way I can describe it is like how detox 'looks' in movies. The sweating, blood pressure swings, nausea, vomiting and dizziness. I started to feel like I was on fire. I became pale. I began to look like I was having a heart attack. I was drenched in sweat; I felt like I was in an oven. I asked for the a\c to be turned on, remember it was January. My heart rate and blood pressure were going up and down. The treatment was over, but I was still labile physically and emotionally. I had now begun coughing. A myriad of new symptoms all at once. More nurses came into the room and the look on their faces when they touched me conveyed absolute bewilderment.

~ Fans ~

The bewilderment stemmed from listening to a man, breathless, complaining of being on fire, yet his skin was ice cold. To me, I was overheating, when someone touched me, I felt like a corpse. I was cold, my skin felt lifeless, I felt like the dead man that the leather satchel toting neurologist warned me that I could become. My body temp was dipping into the low 95's. Not dangerous, but odd. I begged for the temp to be lowered. I was sweating through the sheets. They had to increase my IV drips to keep me from dehydrating, while I pleaded for fans to be brought into my room.

Once again, they caved to my demands, and I was soon surrounded by multiple IV poles with fans attached to each. The noise was deafening to those around me. To me it was soothing. It muffled all the sounds of my monitoring devices. For seconds at a time, I could pretend that I wasn't that ill, yet I continued to lose function. Sleep was still nonexistent. My lung volume edged downward. I was coughing and gasping. I had no idea what day 4 had in store for me, I simply knew that I was losing ground.

~ I Need Pictures ~

Day 4 of ICU would bring day 2 of plasmapheresis. I dreaded it, it made me so sick, but I knew it was my only hope. I lost one of my last shreds of dignity that morning as well. I was now cathed as I lost the ability to empty my bladder. I took solace in the fact that I didn't wet the bed like a child, but nonetheless Guillain Barre had taken something else away from me. It just kept chiseling away at the man I used to be, at the man I was just 4 days ago. They turned on the plasmapheresis machine and I buckled in for another 4-hour ride as respiratory therapy walked in to check my status.

I was steeling my mind against the rigors of plasmapheresis as respiratory therapy mashed the mask against my face. I gave every ounce of my energy to that test. I was coughing and gagging from the exertion. I could feel the sludge in the lower lobes of my lungs. Then I heard the number 2.0. I had failed. I had just lost. It was no longer my fight. I looked at Allie as the pulmonologist, remember the asshole, put his hand on her shoulder and asked if she was ready for what came next in a voice more compassionate than I ever would have thought that he could be capable of producing. He looked at me and I shook my head...no.

I told him no. I begged him, no. I promised that I wouldn't fall any farther. He told me that it was a matter of life and death. He said that I couldn't fall ANY farther. He left shaking his head, confused by this gagging, coughing, fearful and sweaty man. I told Allie that I needed pictures of Serenity and Stoney. I explained that nothing seemed real anymore. That I couldn't see the world outside of that tiny, noisy little room 7 in ICU. I needed an anchor to hold on to, a beacon to light my way through the fight. I needed to be able to look at them. Otherwise, I was terrified that I was going to give up. She left to get them, and I cried as I talked to God.

I cried because I was tired. I cried because I feared a world without me in it to protect my babies. Through teary eyes I explained what he must have already known that I would fight, but I needed his help. That I couldn't do it alone anymore. In the next minutes, for the first time in my life, I found God.

~ The Glow of Faith ~

As my conversation with God continued my thoughts were "directed" to my recent acquisition of anatomical knowledge. I realized my lungs were filling with sludge from my lack of function and general lack of mobility. I was still able to cough so my diaphragm was not completely paralyzed yet. However, I couldn't get the sludge out of my trachea after coughing because I had lost most of my control of my upper throat. I began looking around my room for a solution, not knowing what I was looking for, but then I saw it. I found it. It was literally glowing.

It was a yonker. It's a device that you are familiar with, although at the dentist's office, not likely in the ICU. It is that thing that sucks fluid out of your mouth. In my mind it was glowing. God showed me the answer. I hit the nurse's button and slurred my craziest request yet.

The nurse entered and I began my drunken sales pitch. "I need that." She looked puzzled to say the least. She grabbed my doctor, and they asked my reasoning. I explained, or rather slurred as best that I could, that my diaphragm was still working somewhat, that my lungs were collapsing due to the sludge, that I could cough, but no longer with enough force clear it out of my trachea, that my upper esophageal sphincter being paralyzed would help guard against further vomiting and lower my aspiration risk. I explained that I would force myself to cough to clear my lungs and then shove the yonker down the upper portion of my trachea to manually pull the sludge out of my lungs. I followed my insane pitch with an exhausted eye roll and once again swearing that I wasn't going on a vent. They looked at me, then at each other and said that they couldn't argue with my reasoning but doubted that I would achieve the desired outcome. The doctor gave the nod to the nurse. She walked to me and reluctantly handed me the yonker.

~ 15 Minutes ~

It was now day 5 of ICU, day 3 of plasmapheresis. Allie walked back in with recent wallet sized photos of Serenity and Stoney in frames. They would now live on the table that was in front of me. A constant reminder to not give up. A reminder that they needed their daddy.   Respiratory therapy returned to check me again. The result 1.97. I looked at the clock....it was 8am. I coughed, gagged and shoved the yonker down my throat as the pulmonologist entered my room.

The dark brown sludge gurgled through the device and tubing as I collapsed my head back into my sweat covered pillow. His look was a combination of horror and astonishment. He shook his head and asked how long I thought that I could possibly keep this up. I slurred, "until I lose the use of my hands completely or every 15 minutes until I'm safe." He told me he would have me checked every hour and if I fell to 1.96, I would be vented whether I liked it or not.

My hospitalist entered my room. He sat on the edge of my bed, he had a softer tone, a softer touch to him. He looked at me and told me about a guy. He said that he was about my age and about my build. He told me that he watched him battle Guillain Barre a few years back. He stood up, patted me on the shoulder, grinned a Mona Lisa smile and said, "young man, you're gonna be alright" and looked at the pulmonologist as he left the room.

My schedule was just that, every 15 minutes. I'd cough, gag and grasp this device that I had to visually ensure that I was holding as I could no longer "feel" that it was in my hands then shove it down my throat until I could hear it pulling the strings of sludge through the tubing and collapse again. They turned on the plasmapheresis machine at 9am as I was checked again by respiratory therapy. Was it working?

~ Red and Brown Shift Change ~

The result? 1.97, no better, but no worse. I'd survived another hour without being vented. I restarted my clock as I began to shake, sweat and once again go through the rigors of plasmapheresis. It was at this hour that my shaking got worse, and I rammed the yonker against the roof of my mouth the first of many times. The brown sludge gurgling through the tubing began to take on a red hue. I was starting to cut my mouth and throat, and I was on blood thinners to prevent deep vein thrombosis. It was now 10am. Respiratory was back to check on the crazy guy in room 7.

The result at 10am....1.97 holding. The team kept looking at me in disbelief but nodded and vowed to be back in an hour to recheck. I went back to my schedule. The tubing and reservoir continued to get a deeper shade of red as the cuts in my mouth and throat multiplied throughout the day. Exhausted and listless, I continued and awaited my hourly date with the respiratory therapy team. At 11am I registered at 2.01. It was a victory for not going backward, but no sense of relief as I was pulling up thicker and thicker chucks of red and brown some of which would clog the device itself. I was delirious, but desperately undeterred. I clung to my schedule and my results clung to values around 2.0. The day drug on and it was shift-change for my support system. Allie left and my brother-in-law took over by my side. She didn't need to see what would come next anyway.

~ Giving In to Sleep ~

Chris didn't know what he was walking into that night. I could see that he was horrified by the bloody tubing, but he said nothing as I continued my scheduled self-inflicted assaults. My numbers continued to hang around 2.0. I was ice cold to the touch, sweating profusely, exhausted, shaking, confused and pulling shreds of my mouth and throat out with the sludge. My fingers were bleeding from being cut by my teeth, as my coordination was so bad that I could barely get the yonker to its preferred destination. It was midnight, I had gagged myself about 64 times. Respiratory therapy walked in and tested my volume. I couldn't believe it. It simply couldn't be right.

I was astonished. The respiratory therapist was in disbelief. The reading was 3.3. I did it. I was bloody. I was tired. I was shaking terribly. My face was completely paralyzed. You couldn't tell, but for the first time in days, I tried to smile. I relaxed. I was farther from the ventilator. I had been awake for nearly 5 days. Chris tried to convince me to sleep at least a little bit.

I was still terrified of sleep. Chris begged me to give in and rest, as did the nurses. I laid there for a bit. I wanted one more lung function test. I tested again. It showed 3.4 this time. I agreed to close my eyes and sleep. For the first time in nearly 6 days, I felt confident that I'd wake up okay. I'm told I slept for 45 minutes before I woke up screaming.

~ *Wake Up Call* ~

Pain ripped me into consciousness. I screamed. I couldn't even put together sentences for what seemed like an eternity. I simply screamed in agony. I was finally able to slur the words "my back, my back is getting cut!" It felt as if I was being sawed in half. It felt like the scenes you watch in a movie where a limb is sawed off without anesthesia. The nurses rolled me onto my side, I was still completely paralyzed from the navel down. They stated that they saw nothing. I screamed, "look for the blood!" There was no blood. What they found was disturbing, in a different way, but disturbing, nonetheless.

They found a deep crease. A crease in the sheet. That's all, just a crease. My nerves were on fire. So damaged that a simple crease translated into a level of pain that was previously beyond my comprehension. A level that before that moment, I was unable to wrap my mind around. I writhed and screamed while they awaited a plan of action for pain control at a level that was not anticipated. Seconds felt like years while I begged for something to save me.

There was no saving me. The problem lay in my delicate lung function. You see, decent pain medication suppresses the respiratory reflex of the diaphragm. They couldn't adequately treat the pain without compromising the lung function that I had fought so hard to preserve. Nothing that they could administer made a dent. The pain continued to intensify and had spread from head to toe. It felt as if my skin was being stripped from my arms, legs and face. I could do nothing. They could do nothing.

~ *Just Leave Him* ~

For days, my lung function cycled between 2.5 to 3. It was too risky for adequate pain therapy. My nerves were trying to heal, but their primary purpose was a curse. Your nerves serve a very important purpose, many in fact, but perhaps the most important is protection. Those nerves are a feedback system that you rely upon to keep you from hurting yourself. You sense heat from a stove, pain from a cut and extreme temperatures as a form of self-preservation. My body was reeling and confused. It convulsed in pain. I desperately had my position changed in hopes that it would no longer feel like my bones were pushing through my skin against the weight of my body. I asked for pillows.

Allie and the nurses would shove pillows under various parts of my body trying in desperation to keep me from wailing in pain. Every few minutes it would feel like I had a new compound fracture. It would feel like my legs and face were being burned by an open flame. I held my children's pictures in my trembling hands praying for relief that never seemed to come. Allie was destroyed and exhausted. She wasn't sleeping at home, and she tried to rotate me the best she could. The nurses eventually told her to leave me there as it was too hard to watch and there was no escaping the pain. I languished in the worst pain I'd ever experienced for 3 more days.

~ *Take Anything You Like* ~

The pain continued, but my lungs became stronger. This allowed more liberal use of pain medication. I lost track of the time of day and days of the week for that matter as my body continued to deteriorate from immobility. They brought in an advanced directive at some point. I had clear conversations with Allie before I had ever became ill. Basically organs, anything internal organ-wise was fair game. My answers in ICU, however, were markedly different.

I was in a different state. Unable to feed myself, unsure if I could come back at all. I couldn't read the paper, not that I couldn't put words together, but rather there didn't appear to be any words on the papers placed in front of me. I was now going blind; it looked like a grey sheet of paper. What if I didn't get my vision back? The only one of the 5 senses that was still intact was my hearing. I verbally checked ALL the boxes. Internal organs, eyes, bones, limbs, skin...all of it! I could hear Allie crying and pleading outside the door.

She pleaded with them that she knew what my wishes were and that these were not them. She pleaded that I was not of sound mind because of the trauma and meds. The events of the next morning would settle that argument.

~ *I Like This Room Better* ~

A nurse entered my room for my morning check. She wished me a good morning and asked how I was doing. I responded with, "I like this room much better." She looked at me, grinned softly and said that she was happy that I liked the room better. There was something about the tone of her response that caught my attention. A doctor started to enter the room, and she asked to speak with him outside. Then I heard it. I was wrong, but there was more to it than that.

I heard her tell the doctor that I was under the impression that I had changed rooms, and I hadn't. I was confused. I could make out large objects, it looked different. It felt different. This room has windows. Did my other room have Windows? There was another room, right? No there wasn't. I had studied about this in psyche. I had ICU psychosis. It couldn't be. Could it? Again, time would give me my answer.

Days and many breakdowns later, Allie was sitting with me when I got my answer. My vision was still blurry but improving quickly. My nerves were trying to repair and this led to all sorts of sensations. Then I felt an awful one. I didn't even want to look. I was terrified of what I would see. I looked anyway.

I looked at my legs and arms...spiders! I was covered in them. My heart monitor started spiking. I gasped for breath. Allie asked what was wrong so she could get help. I simply said, "just tell me that they aren't there. If I know that they aren't there, then I can take it" She asked what I was seeing, I told her that it didn't make sense, but I saw spiders crawling all over me. She tried to console me and promised me that there were no spiders. For days I saw spiders on the walls, on the ceiling and on me. I had just enough of my mental faculties left that I knew that they weren't truly there even though I could see and feel them all over me. ICU psychosis is real. I was ashamed to ask for help. I was ashamed that I was too weak mentally to handle it. Allie asked the nurse to give me something to help. He told her I had to ask for it. I refused, ashamed. I suffered for another day, trying to steel my mind. I broke.

I looked up fearfully and the nurse was standing by my bed. My mind being ripped apart between what I saw around the room, now spiders and lizards crawling the walls and all over me. Allie couldn't bear the thought of what I was going through and broke my confidence and told the nurse what I had been seeing. She desperately wanted to do something to help me and that was her only option. The nurse put his hand on my shoulder and said, "Tell me about the spiders brother, it's okay. He started me on meds and the spiders went away. It was the first time in my life that I learned that it is strength and not weakness that resides in asking for help.

~ 92 For a View ~

I was starting to stabilize somewhat. They started talking about moving me to a regular room soon, If I kept my pulse ox above 92. I began watching the monitor constantly. I wanted out of the ICU. I NEEDED to be out of ICU. In my mind, getting out of ICU meant I wasn't in danger of dying anymore. I had to remain at that level for 2 more days then I got to move to a regular room. With 6 hours to go...my monitor started beeping. My pulse ox tumbled before my very eyes.

I panicked. I didn't want them to know, to know that I was slipping backward. I needed out of there. I was crushed. Of course, they came in to check on me, it was the ICU after all. My pulse ox tumbled to the low 80's within minutes. Too far gone mentally for rational thought. I didn't realize that it didn't physically make sense. I wasn't having trouble breathing, no more than usual, for the past couple days. You see, I couldn't feel my hands. The cord of the pulse ox monitor had gotten tangled and had pulled and loosened it from my index finger just enough to affect my readings. The nurse figured it out quickly and reassured me that I was still okay as he saw the tears of fear and defeat roll down my face. The good news...it was now moving time.

I scratched and clawed my way out of ICU. I was being moved to a regular room. This was a major win. I literally breathed easier, just knowing that I was out of ICU. I had less resources at my disposal but somehow felt safer. I was moved in the evening. I didn't turn the TV on. I just lay there. Looking out the window at the night sky. I hadn't seen the outside world in a while. It was beautiful. It felt closer to me, I felt closer to it, even though deep down I knew it was still far from me. I couldn't get out of bed, I couldn't walk or even sit up unassisted, but still, it felt like a big win. It was a win. There was a knock on the door.

~ *Remotely Therapeutic* ~

The overnight nurse entered the room. She said, "I heard that you are quite the fighter." I slurred, "thanks, I am just happy to be here." She took my vitals and talked to me for what felt like an hour. She was kind. I don't remember much of what was said, but it was the first long conversation that I had had without breaking down. I appreciated it more than she would ever know. The next morning brought more pain.

Some low-level physical therapy assessments were on the agenda. The physical therapist set me up on the side of the bed. I screamed in agony. I screamed that my hip was dislocated. It felt like it was being torn out of the socket. They pulled my gown aside to look. They were confused.

It wasn't out of place. In fact, I wasn't even in an awkward position. It was just in a position that I had not been in since going paralyzed. The muscles had atrophied so much, and the nerves were so raw that it felt like I was being drawn and quartered. They apologized as they laid me back flat. My mind raced as I started to comprehend just how long a road lay before me. A road that demanded to be traveled to get some semblance of my life back.

It was now my second night in my normal room. The same nurse, from the night before, knocked and entered the room. "How's the fight going today?" I told her about my hip pain and being a bit dejected about it. She talked a while and explained how the body tightens when we don't use it. It gave me an idea. I still wasn't sleeping well anyway, so I started my own rehab regimen that night.

I had laid flat for weeks. The backs of my legs we like stone. I still couldn't bend them at all on my own, so I reached for my toes. That would loosen me up, but I had no core strength to bend toward my toes, but I had a bed that moved. I couldn't sleep much at all, so I rehabbed on and off all night. Raising and lowering the head of my bed to force the stretching of my hamstrings. It was a wrenching pain in my hands to work the bed remote and I would raise my head until I felt like I was being torn apart, but I just leaned into the pain. I had faith that it would pay off eventually. The back-and-forth motions filled my days and nights for the next week.

~ Remember That One Guy? ~

One evening the hospitalist made his way to my regular room. He peeked in and said, "You see, I told you that you were going to be alright." If I had the ability to grin with pride, I would have done so. Instead, I said, "well you had an advantage sir. You told me about that guy that battled Guillain Barre that I reminded you so much of, so you knew from experience that I was going to be okay." His reply? "I didn't have the heart to tell you, he didn't make it." I was confused, I asked why he brought it up. He said, yes, we looked alike, but he said, "I saw a whole lot of fight in you." He said that gave him hope and he wanted to give me some hope in return when I desperately needed it.

~ *Funds* ~

It was time to start talking about rehab. I was still incredibly weak, but I wanted to get to rehab so that I could get back to school. It was how I kept my kids fed. I fed them with student loan money. Allie was filing for disability for me, but I couldn't depend on that. I didn't want to depend on that. I wasn't built that way. Then my doctor came in to tell me that he had some lackluster news on the rehab front.

My insurance would only pay for one week of inpatient rehab. I needed much more than that, much, much more. He said that he would make some calls and get back with me. It was a defeat. Without the proper support, I could spiral back down, maybe never walk again. A few hours passed and he returned to give me the news.

He called a rehab hospital in a town that neighbored my college of pharmacy, in Clinton, Oklahoma. He and a couple of the ICU doctors make a conference call with the rehab hospital. They pleaded with them to take me as they said that they had never seen anyone fight as hard as I had in ICU. They had a special fund of money set aside each year for pro-bono services for underprivileged patients. They gave all of it to me. It took me from 1 week to 3 weeks. I was estimated to need 2 full months, but the doctors said that if anyone could escape the rigors that lay ahead, it was Stoney Pride. With hopes as high as the odds stacked against me, I was transferred to Clinton.

~ *What's Your Goal?* ~

Once again, they gave Allie and I the option of self-transport, if we agreed to go straight there. I was still hooked up to an IV, still cathed, but I felt sunshine on my skin for the first time in nearly a month. I felt free. I looked at myself in the mirror and didn't recognize my own reflection. I have now lost 50 pounds in just a month. My skin was almost translucent. I could see so many veins in my face. I had been beaten more than half to death, and I still resembled it. It was a stark reminder of how serious this had been and how long the road to recovery would truly be. We didn't speak much on the way to Clinton. What could be said, I was a shell of my former self. Soon, we arrived.

I was wheeled to my room where I waited for Dr. Blakeburn. Allie, both of our children and my sister were there. I hadn't seen my son in weeks, he was so big. He was now around 7 months old. I wanted to hold him so badly, so they placed him in my lap and held him in place. I was still unable to hold my own son. My arms were nowhere near strong enough. I broke down in tears as I tried to support his weight. My sister hugged me which only made me cry harder. I was so upset that I was shaking when the doctor came into the room.

He handed me Kleenex and I apologized for losing it. He was kind and told me that I had lost more than most people could even comprehend in the last month and that I had nothing for which to be sorry. He looked at my son and then looked at me. He asked, "so who is going to walk first?" I slurred, "mmmeee." He said, "I don't know. He is a lot stronger than you are." That was a punch in the gut, but it was true.

He took the standard history and asked what my goal was for my three weeks of rehab. I looked him dead in the eye and slurred, "I'm walking out of here." His eyebrow raised and he asked me to lift one of my feet off the foot supports of my wheelchair. I tried with every fiber of my being to lift my foot, the was no movement at all. Not a flex, not a tremor, nothing. I did not cry. I did not waver. He told me that we may need to reassess that goal later. Again, I slurred, "I am walking out of here." It was late in the afternoon, so no rehab to be endured, but come morning, the work would begin.

~ Sunshine and Razors ~

Bright and early, she walked into my room. She was a cross between Ed Rooney's secretary Grace and nails on a chalk board. She was my day shift nurse. She would later inform me that she had worked at the children's hospital, which would explain why she talked to me in a tone that resembled that of what you would use on an infant. So bright. So cheery. I hated her. God did I hate her. Normally, I wouldn't have hated her, "let's turn that frown upside-down" outlook on life, but Jesus I was in so much pain that I couldn't stand her absolute elation that early in my day. After a week, I found a way to freak her out nicely.

You see at this point it had been 5 weeks since I had shaved. I couldn't stand it anymore. I was still on potent blood thinners because of my lack of mobility, so I was a bleed risk. I asked her to shave. I was denied. I asked, nicely. I was denied. I demanded. I was denied. I was persistent, this they knew. I was also perceptive; this they would soon find out.

I was wheeled to and from my room to my various therapies, whether it was physical, speech or occupational. Then one day I saw it. The supply closet. It housed many things, not the least of which was razors. I was persistent, perceptive and now I needed to be patient.

I spent a couple days studying my nurses and aides as best I could. I had to get the timing right. I asked to stay in my wheelchair and watch TV a little longer one evening. I then waited for my opportunity to make my way to the supply closet. I could nearly hear the mission impossible music in my head as I wheeled my chair to the supply closet to procure my razor. It was the farthest that I had ever moved my chair by myself, but with the motivation of disobedience, you'd be surprised what I could muster. I was in a dead sweat by the time I made it back to my room with my contraband and far too tired to shave before bed. I hid my prize razor in my pillowcase like a shiv in the joint and asked for help to bed. I patted my pillow as I drifted to sleep with a sense of infantile accomplishment because in the morning, we shall shave.

When nurse Sunshine walked in that morning, there I was lathered up, leaned up against the sink, my hand wrapped around a razor like a kindergartner holding a crayon, going to town on my neck and face. She screamed and about fainted. I didn't bleed out and it was totally worth all the trouble that I got into for not getting permission. She screamed for me to stop, and I slurred back at her, "no! I am already halfway finished!" All razors would now be hidden in higher places out the reach of those confined to wheelchairs. I was the story behind a new policy. It was awesome!

~ Urine For a Challenge ~

One of my major goals for the first week was to have my catheter removed as I had now been cathed for 5 weeks. My favorite nurse, who was a kind gentleman, agreed to uncath me at the end of his shift at 7am. He told me that I had until he showed back up at 7pm to pass urine, otherwise they had no choice but to recath me. I assured him that I would have proof in the urinal that I was up to the task. He left, wished me luck and I started pounding water.

As the hours passed by, I felt the urge but couldn't void my bladder. I stayed in my wheelchair all day. I would wheel myself to the bathroom and assume the position. I would just stare at my manhood and beg for the ability to empty my bladder. The clock ticked away relentlessly as I felt my bladder swell by 3pm, panic started to set in.

I begged my body to comply. Minute by minute and hour by hour, I failed. I was distraught when my favorite nurse walked in at 7 to find an empty urinal. The disappointment on his face nearly matched mine. He apologized as he started to re-cath me.

The pain was incredible. My nerves were raw, inside and out, head to toe. It felt as if he was shoving scalding hot shards of glass up my manhood. I was in so much pain that I writhed in the bed and tears streamed down my face, so much so that he cried with me. This would lead to a new symptom that I called OPP.

~ H2OPP ~

Now those folks of my generation are familiar with the song OPP, my acronym meant something else entirely. As the nerves in my manhood started to heal, yes there was pain, but there was something else happening as well. Every single time that my bladder drained into my catheter bag, every single time it drained, I orgasmed. Yes, Ooooooh peepee! For a week solid, I made sure to drink plenty of water. It was the only time that my pain wasn't at a 9 out of 10 on a pain scale. It was absent altogether for about 15 seconds each time that I orgasmed. Thankfully, my face was still completely paralyzed, and I moaned in pain quite a bit, so even if there was someone in the room, they couldn't really tell if I was cumming or going. More water? Yes please!

~ Big Daddy ~

Now let's talk about some shit. No, literally...shit. I've always said that the circle of life has you start in diapers and end in diapers with people wiping your ass when you enter the world and when you leave it. I hadn't accounted for Guillain Barre in my philosophy. GBS added a third episode to that drama. There are few things that will strip you of your dignity like that of having to necessitate the aid of a stranger to wipe your ass for you as a grown ass man. It was humiliating. Hitting the button to get help to get out of bed, getting helped onto the toilet, being left alone to strain for the coordination to only hang my head in defeat as my arms were still partially paralyzed knowing that the nurse would faithfully knock on the door and ask if I was ready to be cleaned up like a toddler. Then one day, Big Daddy made an appearance.

You see, I had been getting a bit better in the coordination department after a couple weeks. As I sat on the toilet, I reached for the toilet paper, wadded it up and successfully reached behind myself and wiped. I truly wiped. The joy, the utter joy that swept over me was palpable. It was like reaching 3rd base with myself. Then there was that faithful knock on the door. The sweet nurse knocked and asked if I was ready to be cleaned up. I slurred excitedly and asked, "have you seen the movie Big Daddy with Adam Sandler?" She confusedly answered "yeeees?" I then proclaimed; "I can WIPE MY OWN ASS!" Just like the kid in the movie. She laughed till she cried and so did I! I was literally taking care of my own shit again! Now on to the task of talking shit.

~ Fuck Speech ~

Speech and vocational rehab were frustrating as uck, uck? Damn it! I still couldn't say fuck. Fucking hated that! They began using electric shock treatments on my face to try to wake it up. I kept having the therapist turn up the voltage. She hated the volts that I had sent through my face, but I couldn't feel it and it barely caused contraction in my face. I was making no gains in speech and my frustration was more than evident. I saw no benefit to it. I felt like I was on a timer and the seconds that ticked away in speech therapy were a waste. I asked if I could change how we were attacking my recovery. My concerns were heard. My feelings were validated. My facial coordination was secondary to my other short and long-term goals. I abandoned speech therapy and opted to double my physical therapy in hopes that I could achieve my goal of walking out of rehab on day 21.

~ Steps of Hope ~

The physical rehab was grueling. It was like a scene out of a geriatric version of Rocky. I was screaming and collapsing from pain and exhaustion. Just the simple acts of trying to stand or roll onto my side would leave me listless. My blood pressure and heart rate would bounce around wildly, but I wouldn't stop, I couldn't stop. I wanted to get home. Going into week two, I stood in a walker. I couldn't feel my legs and they would bow backwards, but I could stand. My physical therapists would wince when they watched me stand. I was hyperextending my knees badly, but damn it felt good to stand up. I hadn't stood in weeks, and I felt so tall, unsteady, but standing, nonetheless. Then I asked if I could try to walk.

They propped me up between parallel bars and had me tied to a harness. I looked up and saw that Allie had walked into the rehab room as I was getting ready to take my first steps. I tried to "show off" to give her some hope. I wanted, no, I needed her to see that her husband was making progress, that I was indeed coming back. I took several very quick steps; it freaked out the staff as I started to stumble. I walked, albeit holding on to bars, but I walked. Allie smiled and cried.

~ Glamping ~

I once again attempted my goal of being uncathed. My favorite nurse had been working on a plan. Bladder training was the gameplan. He would clamp my catheter shut for a few hours at a time. A game plan of clamping, glamping had a whole new meaning. This was done to get my bladder used to the expansion and contraction of normal filling and voiding. There was anxiety when the catheter came out, but less so than the first time. My first attempt to void on my own was a success and a multifaceted relief. I would've never imagined how accomplished pissing into a handheld plastic urinal would make me feel. It did, however, put an end to my OPP. This left me with a unique problem. I still got aroused, but my hands were nearly useless. There was no climax occurring. I confided in Dr Blakeburn. He said that it made sense in terms of healing and the order of things. It hurt though. Maybe Allie could help. I asked.

~ To Hell with Tylenol ~

Now remember, to the touch, I felt like a corpse. I asked her if she'd have sex with me in the hospital bed. Sexual pleasure was the only thing that blunted the pain. She was reluctant, but she complied. With people coming in and out of my room and at all hours unannounced it was risky. I could never climax, but it did relieve my pain while we were having sex. Undoubtedly, we had to have been walked in on a couple of times, laying side by side as my heart monitor would keep spiking and alerting the nurse's station. They had to know what we were doing but were kind enough to never outright tell us that we were busted.

~ *Apartment and My Valentine* ~

There was a gateway drug to the euphoria that was to be my release home. The 'apartment' that was one room over from mine at the skilled rehab facility. It was to be my proving grounds. My ability to show that I could make it on the 'outside.' Yes, I am using prison and parole terminology. It is what it felt like to me. Let me prove that I can be a good boy and be on my own. To ambulate around the apartment would require me to prove that I was completely self-sufficient.

They brought me food that I could try to cook on a stove, in the oven or microwave. I was 30 years old and proving that I could make mac and cheese. Proving that I could get from my wheelchair to the toilet without help. It was exhausting. It was embarrassing. It was necessary.

Valentine's Day arrived and one of my nurses went to the store and got me a card and chocolates for me to give to Allie as a surprise but wait there's more. I and the other patients had an impromptu arts and crafts session. We would be making paper roses that day as a form of therapy. My hands were shit. A therapist placed the tissue paper in front of me and said, go ahead and make Allie a rose. With the most sarcastic tone that I could muster, I slurred, "sure with my little Guillain Barre hands?!" She didn't laugh, but a couple of the others in the room laughed hysterically. It felt good to laugh, I made the ucking rose and Allie cried when I gave it to her. Our two-year-old immediately destroyed it when Allie laid it down, but damn it, I made that ucking rose.

~ 140 Feet ~

My primary focus was on walking. I now had lost 60 pounds. There was no discernable difference between the circumference of my biceps and my wrists. My legs were like sticks and they were barely able to support me. My sister and grandmother were working on getting my deceased grandfather's old hover-round tuned up, but I wanted no part of it. I would walk 10, 20 or 30 feet with a walker. I fell several times in the hallway trying to better my best from the day before. Each time, I was terrified that they wouldn't release me as promised on day 21. I had a goal to get home on time. The facility got approval for another 2 weeks and set a goal of 75 feet of walking with a walker to sign off on me leaving. I didn't want the 2 weeks. I wanted to be home in time for Allie's birthday. It was the only gift that I could give her this year. On day 20, I walked 140 feet and collapsed. It was the hardest that I had fallen to date. I panicked and begged the therapist to not tell the doctor about how bad of spill that I had taken. Tears streaming down my face, I begged him. He told them he had to do so. We had a meeting. I was breathless and felt like I had failed. I was distraught at the thought of another two weeks before being back in my home with my family. I started to beg at the round table but was interrupted. Dr. Blakeburn said, "Stoney, just breath sir, you're getting out of here." On day 21, I got to go home! This victory would be short lived.

~ Church ~

While I battled to get home, Allie battled to keep the roof over our heads. My income, hell, our income came in the form of student loans. Those were not going to come in since I had to withdraw, in fact I had to pay a portion back for that semester because of my withdrawal. Allie started on my disability paperwork as I went paralyzed in ICU. She applied for every benefit she could think of to keep our little family afloat. We were in danger of having our utilities shut off and she begged the operator on the other end of the line for more time. She said that there was nothing the company could do but got her contact information and said she would be in touch soon.

Turns out she spoke to her church about us. About this little family who bet everything on their daddy and husband to make it through school to get them a better life and how he was fighting as hard as he could, but it was going to take time, and their reality was as cold as the temps were that February. The church showed up at our door with diapers, casseroles, toilet paper, gift cards to Wal-Mart and a gas card that she could fill our van up with whenever we needed it. We were not even members of the church, they just showed up to be a force for good for our little family.

~ Home is where the Pain is…For You Bubba, I Can Take It. ~

I got home and was relieved, at first. I once again got to see Allie and my kids every day. They gave me strength. They gave me hope. Then one evening, about 3 days after being home, more of the nerves in my legs woke up. The first thing that shows up is pain, then I get function. I had never experienced this much pain. Not even in ICU. Not even close. I was sitting at the kitchen table while Allie was making dinner.

Suddenly, it felt like my bones were being pulled through the flesh of my feet and legs, then my hands. I simply couldn't hide it. I couldn't stand it. It was completely involuntary. I began screaming in pain. I couldn't even produce words. I couldn't stop screaming. Allie rushed over to me. She'd seen me, heard me in pain before, but not like this. She gave me meds that I could barely swallow because I was writhing in pain so badly. All she knew to do was to try and hold me as tight as she could so that maybe I could feel something besides the agony. This went on for hours before I passed out from exhaustion.

I went to my primary care physician the next day, still sweating in a fight or flight response due to the pain. He increased my pain meds dramatically to no avail. It dulled it, but it still felt like I was being cut with razors from head to toe. It was the hardest month of my life. I then came up with a plan, I would ask to add Lyrica to the litany of pain meds that I was already on to have some sort of quality of life. My doctor obliged reluctantly. It quieted my nerves to the point that I was semiconscious on the couch. I was there, but not really, that afternoon. I couldn't keep track of what Allie was saying. She lost it. She said, "I can take watching you in pain, but I cannot take you being completely out of it. I need you here with me, even if you are in pain." I stopped Lyrica and spiraled back down into unimaginable pain to bring her comfort.

I kept trying to walk. I kept falling onto the floor from the pain that would shoot through my body. My son was learning to walk right alongside me. It was inspiring, it was a bonding experience, not many people get to say that they learned to walk with their son. It was grueling, but in a special way it was a gift. Both of us were trying and falling into and onto stuff. My pain level continued to tick higher and higher. It was pushing me toward my breaking point.

I went on for weeks like that. Then one day, I broke. I lost the will to go on. Allie was napping on the couch and I made my way to the kitchen and pulled myself to my feet to reach my oxycontin. Tears streaming down my face, I knew how many that I had to take to kill myself. I had the knowledge, and I no longer had the will to fight the urge to end it. I poured the whole bottle into my hand and prepared to go to sleep for the last time. Then I felt something on my leg. My son had just begun to walk on his own. He walked all the way across the living room to the kitchen and he wrapped his little arms around my leg. When I looked down at him, he smiled up at me. I put the pills back into the vial. He saved my life. I looked at him and said, "for you, bubba, I can take it."

~ Pickles ~

The impact of chronic illness on relationships cannot be overstated. It can be cataclysmic under the best of circumstances, ours were far from the best circumstances. Going from the person that was leaned on to the person doing the leaning was hard on both of us. It is not something that you can prepare for, not something you can imagine, not something that you even want to fathom. I can recall a pivotal moment. I was still wheelchair bound, and Allie was in the kitchen, and I was at its edge. She wanted pickles, she loved them. I was always the designated jar opener. However, I could barely grasp the jar, let alone open it. She struggled with the lid and instinctively turned to me. Both of our shoulders dropped simultaneously. She said, "it's okay, I've got a plan." She tapped the jar's lid on the edge of the counter to loosen it. Still nothing. I sat in my wheelchair unable to help her get to the simplest of pleasures. She tapped it again and the jar shattered and broke into what seemed like a hundred pieces.

She screamed the most helpless anguished scream that you can imagine and collapsed to the floor and yelled, "I just wanted pickles." She sobbed on the floor for what felt like an eternity. I couldn't get out of my chair to comfort her. I couldn't help her clean up the shards of glass. Our dynamic had shattered long before the jar did, but it was so symbolic of how broken our life had become because of my illness and disability.

~ *Torn Sheets* ~

The dynamic went deeper than pickles. As my nerves continued to heal, I continued to suffer more and more pain. Everything hurt, everything. Touches might feel like compound fractures one day or like a lighter being held to my skin the next. Sleeping was nearly impossible. If I did manage to fall asleep, if the sheets moved, it would feel as if my skin was being peeled off me. It led to fear of hurting me by simply touching me. It led to more distance between us. It felt like I was being torn apart, but we were being torn apart as well. It is not easy to watch someone in pain and not be able to do much, if anything, about it. For fear of robbing me of any sleep that I could manage and fear of hurting me more than I already was, we began sleeping apart most nights. The toll that my illness took on each of us was incalculable. I couldn't be the man she fell in love with, I went to war every day with pain and fear. The pain was physical and mental, the fear of not ever being the person that she fell in love with again was ever present. I remember being up one night watching House M.D. It was the episode where he was on the bus with Amber. He was in between worlds, between life and death. She told him to get off the bus and essentially go back to his old life. He said that he couldn't. When she asked why, he replied, "because it doesn't hurt here." Those words broke me, I sobbed for what felt like hours. I feared the battles that still lay before me. Meanwhile, Allie faced battles of her own.

~ *Bruises* ~

Bruises, not mine, but Allie's. If you recall, she had to have emergency gall bladder surgery while she was pregnant with our son. There were risks involved with that surgery. Our son is amazing, but he was difficult when he was little. While her husband was disabled and screaming in pain, her son was inconsolable too. I was an irritable baby, my mother told me stories that I cried for years, that nothing worked to soothe me. My son was following in my footsteps, but it fell on Allie when he was little. I still wasn't strong enough to hold him as I was still physically flailing myself. All the usual fixes and tricks didn't work to calm him. We would later learn that he had autism. Allie would take him to the store and come home covered in bruises from a toddler. The world overwhelmed him and while it was overwhelming him, she held him. She was terrified that he wouldn't ever return the affection; she loved on him and held him despite his flailing. It exhausted her, how could it not. This was not the life that we had envisioned. I am convinced that it is because of her unwavering love, cuddles, hugs and caresses that we have one of the kindest and most gentle young men ever to walk the earth. Allie was amazing with our babies when I was at my sickest. She loved being a mommy to little ones and poured as much energy into them as she could to give them some sense of normalcy. It was energy better spent; she could make a difference with them much more so than with me. Her touch may be agonizing to me because of my nerve pain, but her touches and caresses would comfort them. I will forever be grateful for how she wrapped her arms around our babies while I battled my way back in those early days, months and years.

~ *Parallel Bars* ~

There was a park near our home. It had parallel bars on the playground, much like I used in rehab, but now I could use them while I watched my babies enjoy the park. I can remember my daughter walking between the bars in front of me saying, "like this daddy, you can do it." My daughter eagerly tried to teach me to walk, to encourage me to do the very thing that I had taught her to do not so long ago. I would sway back and forth and bang my hips into the bars, frustrated, yet grateful to have the privilege of being back with my family while I was literally finding my footing. We would come to the park often and I would eventually graduate to making my way around a walking trail with Allie. I was using a walker, then a cane. Sometimes wobbling, sometimes falling, but always trying desperately to get back on the path to building a better life for my family.

~ *Because He Says So* ~

The pain continued. My recovery continued as well. I could now walk with a cane. It was early May when I called to reenroll in pharmacy college. I was told no. My counselor advised me that I was not well enough. That I was still too sick, too disabled to be able to take on the rigors of pharmacy school. I explained that I couldn't feed my kids without student loans BECAUSE I was disabled. He explained that he couldn't "save" me WHEN I failed out of pharmacy school. That I would not get any leeway. I wouldn't receive mercy from the academic committee. I became enraged, cussed him and told him that just because HE wasn't strong enough to pull it off, didn't mean that I wasn't. Allie heard the exchange and walked out of the house. She headed to the school.

She burst into the main office of the college of pharmacy and screamed for the Dean and the admissions counselor. She cussed the dean, the counselor and anyone within view. She dressed them all down without hesitation. The quote that I heard later was, "if Stoney Pride says he can do something, he can fucking do it. Do you understand that? He can do it, because he says so. Because he's Stoney Fucking Pride!" They enrolled me without further discussion…

~ *A Cane, Cans, a Fan and Curves...My Return to Pharmacy College* ~

I started out the door of our house and looked down at my cane. I threw it into the corner. Allie asked me what I thought I was doing. I told her that I didn't want to look sick, so I wasn't taking my cane. She said, "baby you look sick either way. Take your damn cane." I left my cane anyway. I was welcomed back to school with a combination of open arms and "poor guy" looks. To be truthful, I was expected to fail. I was the underdog and lots of people were rooting for me to simply pass with the bare minimum. My hands still barely worked. I had accommodation for extended time and if necessary, oral examinations. I opted for the extended time to start as I didn't want to draw more attention to myself than I already had so far. I sat in my first class. I made it about 5 minutes into an old school slide presentation, before it hit me.

I hobbled to the hallway and vomited in the nearest trash can. My vertigo was so bad that I got motion sickness from watching transparencies slide across the projector. This was not a good start. I went back into the classroom to the stares of my classmates and the professor, as everyone could hear me hurling in the hallway. I made it through the first class, but I was in so much pain that I was drenched in sweat. My next accommodation was peculiar. A fan. My body continued to remain in fight or flight for a year. Which made me sweat profusely on a constant basis. I asked my professors for permission to use a small fan, they were concerned that other students might complain about the noise. No one complained, to quote my friend Donnie, "damn it, give the man a fan we don't care." I got the okay for a small fan that I took from class to class so that I didn't sweat all over the table.

My first exam was in pharmaceutics, pharmacy math. It was math done by hand. I asked for extra sheets of paper as I still wrote like a preschooler, I was still relearning how to write. I also asked for extra time, and it was granted to me. I didn't require extra time but turned in a novel's worth of scratch paper to show my calculations. I was in disbelief when the grades were posted in the hallway the next morning.

I set the curve in a class of 70 of the best and brightest students. I got hugs, high fives and atta boys from everyone. Everyone was shocked, including me. I had a lot of cheerleaders in the form of my classmates. I continued my journey. I would fall down flights of stairs, I'd fall up flights of stairs, I fell into the drinking fountain when I lost my balance because of vertigo. I continued to puke in trash cans. I continued to set the curve in nearly every subject. The cheers got less and less. The sick old guy was starting to make the young kids look bad. I had a secret weapon that they didn't know about.

~ *The Nickname* ~

Pain. Pain was my secret weapon. How was that my secret weapon? I was in so much pain that I literally only slept about two hours a night for most of my pharmacy college career. I shook. I sweat. I would writhe. I did not sleep. So, I figured that if I wasn't sleeping, then I would read and study. I studied more than anyone else. At my doctor's appointments, I would be asked to rate my pain. My doctor begged to increase my pain meds as he couldn't stand to see me live at an 8 out of 10 on a pain scale. I refused. I was afraid that if I treated my pain with more than 240mg of oxycontin that I wouldn't retain what I studied. So, I lived in pain to learn and retain what I needed to graduate. My first three semesters back from Guillain Barre were 4.0, 4.0, 4.0. I did not fail, I thrived, somehow, I thrived. I was in and out of the hospital each semester. I studied medicinal chemistry while receiving IVIG to stop a relapse. Doctors shook their heads. Everyone shook their heads. I was cranky. I was short with everyone. I set the curves. I was flat out mean for the first time in my life. I walked with a limp. It earned me the nickname Dr. House.

I fell everywhere I went. I fell at home. I stepped on a blanket that had a crease in it. It felt like my foot was cut in two. I hit my head on the door frame on the way down. Allie screamed at me each time that I fell. She said it was out of "love and fear." She "loved" me each time I faltered. She was getting tired of being with the sick guy, I could tell.

Soon, I had managed to survive long enough to make it to my experiential rotations, which was my last year of pharmacy school. I now had the opportunity to work in pharmacies of all types. This would be my first attempt to be on my feet for an extended period. Once again, I went back into fight or flight. I sweat so badly from the pain that I had to have paper towels handy to blot the sweat from my face, at all times. It was embarrassing, but manageable. What came next scared everyone.

I went to fill my monthly pain meds, and it wasn't covered any more. That was the year that Medicare, I was declared permanently disabled, stopped paying for extended-release opiates. Allie called the school in a panic. We couldn't afford it, not even close. I was so close to the finish line, and she was worried that I would crumble, hell I was worried too. The cost was nearly a thousand dollars a month. I had 4 months to go. My counselor called me to let me know that the school was going to be doing a fundraiser to help pay for my meds so I wouldn't crumble so close to the finish line. I refused to accept the help and told them to cancel the fundraiser. I decided to come off pain meds cold turkey. I was already in pain. How much worse could it be? Everyone around me absolutely lost their mind over my decision. I came off the meds on a Saturday morning.

~ *You Are Real?* ~

I knew the pharmacology. Opiate withdrawal is not fatal, but it is highly unpleasant. For someone who had been on high dose opiates for as long as I had been, the symptoms could last for a month. Diarrhea, vomiting, sweating, tremors, mood swings and of course the most feared by me and my loved ones, a dramatic increase in an already intolerable amount of pain. I chewed tums like they were candy to stave off the diarrhea. I was already sweating, and I already tremored. I was already moody. I braced myself for the pain. It would hit me Sunday morning by my calculations. I fell asleep on what I was sure was going to be my last relatively decent night for a long time.

I woke up Sunday morning confused. The pain wasn't worse. I rationalized that I was a slow metabolizer and that the worst would hit on one of the following mornings. Monday came and went, and I wasn't worse. Tuesday and Wednesday came and went and something surprising happened. I wasn't worse, I was better. As each day drug on, my pain did not worsen. It turns out that I had fallen victim to the side effect of hyperalgesia when on opiates long term. In 1% of people, opiates start causing pain instead of relieving it. Had I tried to treat my pain to a lower level when the doctor begged me to do so, I would have learned it earlier. I was still in a great deal of pain, but now my mind felt sharper than ever. It was a bizarre win, but a win none-the-less. The only thing more bizarre than this is what happened on my last rotation.

I had made it to my final rotation and was feeling as good as I had since Guillain Barre. It was a hospital rotation, which meant that my partner and I got to show some first-year students around and show them what they could expect during their final year. Sara and I waited patiently by the elevator for the first years to arrive. Two nervous young men got off the elevator and shook Sara's hand and introduced themselves. They then shook mine, I said, "I'm Stoney Pride and I will show you guys around." I was taken aback by their reply.

"You're real?" I said, "yeeeaaah?" They then proceeded to tell me that everyone thought that I was a ghost story. That the professors tell a story of a student that nearly died from Guillain Barre. That he would puke in trash cans, he fell down flights of stairs, studied while laid up in the hospital multiple times a semester. That no student ever had an excuse to fail a test, because Stoney made straight A's when he shouldn't have even been able to make it to class period. I was a ghost story. I was a ghost that would graduate Magna Cum Laude the following month. I grinned with the side of my face that allowed me to do so and said, "boo!"

~ Graduating to Facebook ~

I scratched and clawed my way to graduation and accepted a job offer in East Texas. I got a hefty sign-on-bonus that allowed me to buy a home in a lakeside community. This was our opportunity to get ahead for the first time in our marriage. I passed my board exams without issue and started my career. I was terrified, but excited. This is what I had worked so hard for all these years. It should've been the happiest time of our marriage, but it wasn't.

The pain for me was still ever present. I was never really the same after I got ill with Guillain Barre. I wasn't happy-go-lucky like I was when we met, how could I be. I was exhausted, my body still fighting me every step of the way. I was short, I will admit that. Once I became ill with Guillain Barre in 2007, I was no longer the man that she fell in love with just a few years prior. We didn't get the years of foundation that lots of couples get before the, for better or worse and sickness and in health parts of the vows were truly put to the test.

I was stressed. I was scared, scared of relapsing at any moment. It was like imposter syndrome, outwardly seemingly like I had everything under control, but inside I was terrified that everything could be ripped away again in a matter of hours like it had been when I ended up in ICU in pharmacy school. On my better days, I oozed confidence that was interpreted as cockiness and on my worst days, those incited worry and uncertainty. I tried my best to cope, to be anything and everything that folks needed me to be at any given moment. I was simply not the man that she fell in love with all those years ago.

I use humor to cope with stress. I use humor to distract me from pain. I use humor when I am happy. In short, I use humor ALL the time. Allie would swing by the pharmacy all the time in the beginning. If I was laughing with a female, I must be cheating on her. I never cheated. Not once. Not ever. She was insecure, although she had no reason to be. She was beautiful and I doted on her every chance that I got. I left notes for her. I bought her roses on my way home from work just because it was Wednesday. If I left for work 10 minutes early, my phone would ring, and she'd accuse me of having sex in the parking lot. Her family members had a history of instability. They were incapable of being happy, incapable of winning, winning scared them to death. I tried harder and harder. I showered her with affection and gifts. The good days were awesome, but the bad days were terrible. I never even so much as held another woman's hand throughout our marriage. Then I did the unthinkable, I accepted friend requests from my two ex-wives.

This lasted for about two weeks. She accused me of wanting to get back together with Misty. She accused me of loving Misty more than her. I refuted the allegation, although she was my first love. She told me that I could only pick one ex to be friends with on Facebook. I knew it was a test. I deactivated my entire account. This enraged her even more because she couldn't out me for still having feelings for Misty. I did still have feelings for Misty, but she was married again and had another child. That ship had sailed. I was allowed to have a Facebook account a year later. But I had to use my middle name, not my real last name and had to be completely private and she had the password so she could track whether I had any contact with Misty. She feared my first love. Although she was friends with her exes on Facebook because it would be rude not to be, and she might need them for a reference when and if she returned to the job market.

I did think of Misty. Her profile was completely open. I checked it from time to time. She looked happy and I dare not interfere with that. I missed her, but I never acted on those feelings. Then I got a call from my sister out of the blue. The kind of call that I had gotten before.

~ *The Cruiser and Keystone Light* ~

My grandmother was dying and wasn't going to make it through the night. I was 5 hours away. I had my sister hold the phone to her ear. I told her that I was coming to say goodbye and please hold on as I couldn't have a repeat of what happened with mom. We raced toward Oklahoma City. We got within 20 miles and my phone rang. It was my sister. I didn't even say hello. I said, "I am too late again huh?" She passed away. I was getting good at being just a little late where dying relatives were concerned. I was heartbroken again. I had a 3-day weekend, so we stayed at my grandmother's house to handle her estate.

She was extremely frugal. She was a great-depression kid. We were not incredibly close when I was a child, hell even as an adult. However, after she became widowed, continued to fight cancer and I got sick in pharmacy school, we bonded like never before. She told me that she liked PT Cruisers. She thought that they were cute. She wouldn't buy a car that she really wanted while she battled cancer, it boggled my mind. I knew she had money, not exactly how much, but I knew she had enough. I scoured car lots and found a used one for seven grand. She refused. She said that she couldn't bring herself to do it. She said she might need the money, that my sister or I might need something. When we opened her checkbook on the weekend of her passing, we found that she had $108K in her primary checking. I hated that she didn't get that car. We looked over her stocks and did the math and I was going to walk away with around 90k when it was all said and done. I will never forget Allie turning on the old stereo and trying to dance with me. She was a little too happy for my liking. I said nothing so as not to offend her.

My grandmother had fancy clothes and unlike my mother, she had all her final arrangements laid out to a T. She spoke to my sister and I about what she wanted to wear to be put to rest, pajamas. She said that the road she had traveled had been long and the fight with cancer was hard. She said, "I am ready to be comfortable." She was adorable in her little pajama cap.

My sister asked if I wanted to speak at the graveside. I initially said no. When the time came, my sister had her's prepared and asked me one more time. Once again, I declined. My sister spoke, she was eloquent and politically correct, as she always had been. She took her seat beside me once more and I patted her on the leg, grinned and stood to speak as a memory had sprung to mind.

I stood by her casket and did my thing, I just started talking. The memory was from when I was still very ill from Guillain Barre and trying to finish school. Allie, the kids and I were visiting her one weekend and she decided to burn some brush. I was barely walking, but I wasn't about to let her do it by herself. It was just her and I in the backyard and she looked around suspiciously and asked, "Do you want a beer?" Mind you that she was very strait laced, and I had NEVER seen her drink in my life. I hid my shock and said, "hell yeah." The funeral attendees grinned as I recounted how she secretly scurried in the house and returned with two cans of Keystone Light of all things. She winked at me as we shared our first beers together and I just started laughing. She asked what was so funny. I replied in my best Jeff Foxworthy, "if you can barely walk from being paralyzed and you and your cancer fighting grandma are pouring gasoline on a pile of burning brush, youuuuu might be a redneck." Everyone laughed and wiped away their tears for a moment. It was the first time that I cried at a funeral since my mother's passing that the tears were for the departed and not from the memories of my mother.

~ *Better to Be Pissed Off Than* ~

We were set up to win, financially at least. I started upgrading the house as she wanted. I tore through cash quickly, but she was happy. She wanted a mommy makeover as the kiddos had done a number on her body. I gave her the green light and signed a check for a little over $20k. I waited on her hand and foot. I will never forget the first day I went back to work the day after her surgery. She called me in a panic saying that she couldn't urinate. She asked if I felt comfortable cathing her to relieve the pressure. I called across the street to the medical supply pharmacy. I asked if they sold cath supplies, the pharmacist knew me, he replied with a long yeeessss. I flew home and she was laying on a towel on the floor. I knew anatomy but had never cathed anyone. As Batman said in the Lego Movie...first try! Let's just say that I had to change clothes before I went back to finish my shift.

I kept racing home at lunch to make sure she had everything that she needed. Once she was healed, once she didn't need me as much anymore, we started fighting again. Once again, I was accused of cheating. I never did. She called me one evening while I was at work to tell me that she had gotten pulled over, but didn't get a ticket. I was happy that she didn't cost me any more money. She thought she hung up, she hadn't.

I said hello, but all I heard was her excitedly telling her friend that a highway patrolman just asked her out when he pulled her over. My knees buckled as I stood at my work computer. I confronted her when I got home. Now I was being called the crazy spouse. She said she didn't say yes and that I had nothing to worry about. He knew she was married by the registration on the car. He was a well-known douchebag, a civil servant, he was her type. I trusted her, as she still couldn't have sex for another 2 weeks due to her mommy makeover. The night before her all clear for sex I made advances toward her, but she said she was still not ready.

~ Seaworld ~

We fought the next day, and she had homework to do, she was getting her education now. So, I decided to take the kids to Sea World as I had the weekend off and admittedly, I knew she wanted to go as well. Passive aggressive, yes, but better than having a screaming match. I called her from Sea World at the end of our day and she was making tacos at her friend's house. She sent pics and videos from the very friend's house that she bragged to about getting asked out by the highway patrolman. I got a hotel room with the kids, and I took them to a movie, but I got a bad feeling. I called her phone, but it went straight to voicemail. I checked out of the hotel and started driving home a day early. When I arrived at midnight, she wasn't home. She didn't answer her phone until 2 am. She was with the highway patrolman. She saved her $20k mommy makeover for him.

It turns out that she had sex with him multiple times before I left with the kids to go to Sea World that week. She had originally told me that she wanted to lose her newfound "virginity" to me. I asked why him, her reply, "I just wanted to make sure that it wasn't you," in the coldest reply that I had ever received. She told me that he was in better shape than I was and that I wasn't attractive anymore. It was inflicting pain for the sake of inflicting pain. I was devastated, I had cheated death. I spent my inheritance just to make her smile. I gave serious thought to suicide for the second time in my life. I wanted a divorce but was not willing to go without seeing my children every day. Afterall, I was the one that studied with them, I was the classroom parent, I packed their lunches, I drove them to school. I did it all and loved every minute of it. I clung to her. I begged her to stay. I told her that I forgave her. I showed her more love and affection than ever. She continued to accuse me of cheating. I never did.

~ *Stupid Cars* ~

I was so terrified of losing someone who didn't want me anymore. How terrified? Well, we lived in a rural area. The kind of community where everyone knows everyone's business and what they drive. I was so scared of him seeing her driving around town that I bought her a new car, to buy me a few weeks of him maybe not recognizing her when she was out and about. I bought myself one too. Not thinking about what would happen next.

I was driving home from work and had just had a helluva day. I was on edge and not really paying attention to how fast I was driving. All the sudden, I see a highway patrolman behind me with his lights on. I pulled over and looked in the review mirror as he got out of his car. It was him, the man who fucked my wife.

He made it to my window and froze a bit when he realized who he had just pulled over. I said, hey Dave. He took my license and registration and went back to his car. I texted Allie and informed her of the situation. She panicked and begged me to stay calm and not get myself arrested by losing my shit.

He returned to my window and said, "I am going to let you off with a warning." I spotted his bodycam and grinned. I said, "well I figure that's the least you can do since you've been fucking my wife." He stood there in a daze holding my license and registration in his hand as the gravity of the situation began to rush over him. I said, "can I have my documents now, or do you want to talk about Allie?" He handed me my license and just walked away. That was the best I had felt in quite some time, for once, I made him uncomfortable, and that little jab let him know a bit more about me.

~ Running From My Problems ~

The anger that I felt was not healthy. I was in debt and took on more and more responsibilities to keep up with her tastes. I decided to try to start jogging. I had not done so since before Guillain Barre. It was exhausting, but I kept at it. It gave me some peace that I desperately needed. It gave me some quiet. It gave me solitude. It gave me an outlet for stress and a way to lose weight and hopefully become more desirable to Allie.

The cop still wanted my wife, not that he wanted her, but he wanted my house and her alimony. He would walk by my pharmacy and just smile at me hoping that I'd divorce her, and he could swoop in and capitalize. So, I ran my rage away every morning for years. I dropped from 250 to 195. I ran half marathons on a regular basis. I was in better shape than I ever thought possible. I was starting to regain my confidence. We started to get along better. She always showed me more affection when I weighed less than 210 pounds. Then the unexpected happened.

~ Baby No ~

It was a Friday. My district manager showed up at the pharmacy. It wasn't unusual to be checked up on by upper management. Then I got pulled aside. I got laid off, effective immediately. I dressed him down verbally. He apologized and said he had struggled with it for weeks. I said he owed me two weeks. He agreed to my pleas.

I remember driving home and calling Allie. I usually called her to see if I needed to pick up anything. I just said one thing, "I just got laid off." She said, "That is impossible, you're a pharmacist. I walked into the house, made dinner for everyone as I usually did and then sat down at my computer and typed CVS.com. She said, "Baby no, you won't survive it." CVS is a torturous place to work. I knew she was right but I had no choice. Afterall, between the house remodel and the mommy makeover, we had no savings. I applied for a manager position over an hour away. I got called the very next morning and interviewed on the spot over the phone. I got hired sight unseen. All my coworkers worriedly congratulated me for landing on my feet.

~ Longview....and the Bible ~

We had placed the house up for sale before I had got laid off. There had been no rush, but now there was more motivation. I had taken on more stress and a combined commute of 3 hours a day. Finally, our house sold as my fatigue was setting in. I chose to move us to Longview as I couldn't bear the thought of our autistic son on a bus in Tyler, Tx. I had some friends in Longview and my favorite east Texas bowling center was there as well. It would put some distance between her and the highway patrolman too. It was a win-win. Another fresh start.

We found a giant home with a pool, bought two new cars, got two English bulldogs outfitted the game room, new furniture, and I got my bowling pro shop set up in the garage. Every 'thing' was perfect. We, on the other hand, still were not. I just got a feeling as she was acting a little off. I checked her phone records, and she was sending pictures to an unknown number and texting that number only when I was at work or bowling league. It started when she went to a hockey game with one of my former cashiers. She gave her number to another man and hung all over him right in front of one of my employees. Once again, making me look like a fool at work. She denied it of course, but it occurred. I forgave her again and tried harder still. Then something happened that made her lose her mind. My Facebook messenger dinged while I was writing a paper for my master's degree. She was standing over me, I hadn't heard from this person in 15 years, it was Misty.

Allie immediately said, "what the fuck does she want? Oh, I know.... you!" I opened the message that started with Hey stranger and went on to tell me that she had somehow ended up with my deceased mother's bible, she was preparing for her third marriage. Perhaps her third marriage would go better than mine. She had found my mother's bible while going through storage. She asked if I wanted it, and if so, she could mail it to me if I gave her my address. Allie lost her mind; she told me that I wasn't allowed to have it back and that the only reason that she held on to it was to try to steal me back when the time was right. She told me that if I replied nicely at all that she would kick me out and that I would never see my kids. It crushed me to be short with my first love, but I had snooped at her profile, and she looked happy. It looked like I had no chance as she was gearing up to marry her third husband. I replied, "nah I'm good." It killed me for weeks. Allie was mad about it for months. I would check Misty's profile periodically from then on. She always looked happy with him, and I dared not do anything to ruin her happiness, after all I told her to find me if things fell apart for her all those years ago. Did she even remember that? Besides, I was getting sick again and she deserved a better version of me than I had to offer, and she was right at Denny's when we talked years before, I couldn't bear the thought of breaking up my family no matter how unhappy that I was in the marriage.

~ Hi. I'm Negan ~

I started to get sicker and sicker with each passing day. Nothing specific, not yet, but I would take time off from work when I could. I began watching The Walking Dead. I became less social to rest in the evenings. I used to go to all sorts of local functions, but now my wife would go on her own. This always begged the question, where's Stoney? I was the 'entertainer' between the two of us. Socially, I was the draw. Soon, the rumors began to swirl that there was trouble in what others might have thought was paradise. We had attended a Halloween fundraiser for a local art museum the year before and won best costume going as a steampunk couple and she wanted to go again, but I was not feeling well when tickets were being sold. I told her to go without me. This led to a question on her messenger.

Her friend's boyfriend asked her if she was going to be showing a lot of cleavage. I had only met him once and immediately labeled him a douchebag. Allie originally argued, but when she showed me the message, she admitted that I was right all along. She didn't play into it; with our history she begged me to trust her. I did, but I hatched a plan. Allie agreed that it was genius.

Their table was full, but I messaged my friend Joe and asked if he still had a spot at his table. He did, I offered to pay for the hundred-dollar plate, but once he learned why I was coming, he said, "watching what is going to happen would be more than worth the hundred bucks."

I overnighted a Negan cosplay costume complete with Lucille and kept my arrival a secret. I would arrive fashionably late to ensure that all the important folks would get to witness what was about to happen. You see, the theme was over the river and through the woods. He dressed up as the grandmother with little wolf ears and all to go with his purple moo-moo and pajama cap. I arrived and strolled to his table to find him exactly where I wanted him to be, right between my wife and his girlfriend with a big grin on his face. He looked at me in a leather jacket with a barbwire covered bat on my shoulder and his eyes widened. I said, "hi, I'm Negan." He exclaimed, "that is not the theme! That is not the theme!' I grinned and said, "I've never been much for following rules, but I dig your pajamas." As I rested the bat, Lucille, on his shoulder and just walked to my table and sat with my buddy Joe.

I could hear him from 3 tables away screaming, "I look stupid, I look so stupid!" He ripped his costume off in disgust. I ruined his evening. He sensed the blood in the waters of my marriage and tried to capitalize. It was glorious. I just grinned and sipped my drink. It remains my favorite swipe of a credit card that I have ever made. I still have the Negan costume cosplay and have worn it every Halloween since and in a few Tik-Toks here and there, a reminder that sometimes it takes a bully to put another in its place and that not all heroes wear capes. I always knew Michael. I always knew.

~ *My Own Father? Really?* ~

I was sitting on the back porch when my phone rang. It was my sister. We weren't terribly close, but she would check in on me from time to time. I answered and said, "What's up sis? She said, "it's dad." My heart sank, thinking that he had had another heart attack, but unfortunately it was much worse. When I heard the news, I did not argue. I believed her. My head fell into my hands. Allie asked what happened, I was still on the phone, I told Allie that dad had molested a child and attempted to molest a second. Allie flew into a rage and yelled that the kids were lying. I remained calm, as did my sister, and just accepted it as the truth. He was always broken, but we NEVER thought that he would do anything like this, never. Then my mind began to race. He was alone with our daughter when she was little. I became incensed.

When our daughter was in pre-k she kept having accidents at school, one of the tell-tale signs of abuse. He was only around her a couple times, but that is all it could take. I became enraged as I was molested as a child. He saw what it had done to me. How could he do it? Knowing what I went through as child. I called him from the parking lot before I went to work the next day. He answered the phone. I simply asked, "is it true?"

His reply? "Well, that's what they say." It was all that I needed to hear. It was true, he just didn't have the balls to say it. I told him that I was beyond disgusted and hurt. That he could watch his own son go through it and do it to another child. He sat in silence. Then I asked a question that could not go unanswered. "Did you touch my daughter?" He swore that he hadn't. I told him that it didn't matter. I told him that he would never lay eyes on me or any of my family again. I said, "I will see you at your funeral," and hung up the phone.

~ *Thanksgiving* ~

My mother passed away while we were on bad terms, and it still wrecked me to that day. This, however, was different. This was egregious. This was inexcusable. I could live without talking to him again. My conscience would be clear. I had opportunities over the years to see him again but kept passing on the chance to do so. Then one Thanksgiving six years later it happened.

He had been in an assisted living facility for about 2 years and his health was declining. We came up to visit my family, in Oklahoma. Everyone was standing around talking in my sister's home and I asked where the nursing home was located. It was not far, within a few miles. I grabbed my coat, and several family members stood between the door and me. They were afraid of me losing my temper, afraid of me hitting him out of anger, afraid of me losing my license to practice, afraid of me losing my ability to provide for my family. I assured them that I could handle it and that it was for me, not for him. I wasn't going to take the chance of carrying around the burden of losing another parent without saying goodbye in person. Against their better judgement, they let me go alone.

I arrived at the nursing home, and it had the familiar smell of a hospital. I approached the desk and asked where his room was located. I got an odd look from the lady at the desk, and I explained that I was his son, and she nodded and cautiously gave me the info, almost as if she had heard why I had never stopped by before. I approached the room with an eerie calmness about me. I could smell the stench from the hallway. I knocked on the door and I heard his voice say, come in.

~ *Breaking My Word* ~

I stepped inside and saw a shell of a man sitting in a chair. His pajamas were stained. His nails were long and yellow. Unkempt is not the word. I don't think there is an adequate word for his state. He was no longer Superman. He had decayed, profusely. I saw him deteriorate after mom passed, but this was altogether different. You could have placed him under an overpass, and it would have suited him better than being in a nursing home. My eyes watered not from sadness, but from the smells. I asked him, "how are you doing today sir?"

He said that he was doing alright and that they had been taking pretty good care of him. I asked if he needed anything. He didn't think that he did. "No snacks? No cigarettes?" He said that he had everything that he needed but thanked me for checking in with him and that I was kind for asking and offering. He didn't recognize me. His own son had become a stranger in the last six years. I could have left, and he would have never even known that I had broken my word of his never laying eyes on his son again. Then I spoke once again.

I said, "I told you that you would never see me again." His eyes grew large with disbelief. "SON!" he exclaimed, "my God my son you are here!" I told him that I hated him for what he had done, but I appreciated the father that he was to me and my sister. I told him that the visit was not for him, but for me. What he did was unforgivable, but I couldn't carry the guilt of not saying goodbye in person to my last parent. The wonder left his eyes, and he nodded in silent understanding. I offered him anything he wanted from the store once more, but again he declined. He struggled to his feet and approached me. I gave him a hug and said I cannot forgive you; I told him that was God's job, not mine, and that I hated what he did, but more than that I hated that I still loved him. He said, "I understand, and I love you son." I left his room not knowing whether either of us were better for having the visit.

~ Surviving Miles at a Time ~

One of the reasons for her infidelity always seemed to point to my lack of manliness. As always, I tried to win her affection and loyalty. I was a firm believer that my distance running kept my immune system in check. However, she kept mentioning that she wanted me buffer. So, I attempted just that, I began lifting weights. Within 2 weeks, I hurt my back so badly that I could no longer run. I gained weight fast and I began having bizarre symptoms that my doctors couldn't pinpoint. Allie said that I was paranoid and that I just had PTSD, but I didn't feel right. I hadn't run for a year and then one morning I woke up at 3am feeling like I would have a heart attack if I didn't run. I told Allie and ran into the darkness of east Texas. I ran 10 miles in the cold with no training at 240 pounds. I only stopped myself because I was going to be late for work if I didn't. I went to the doctor the next day. The most likely culprit? Adrenal cancer.

It would be a month before the testing would be complete. In the meantime, my blood pressure was going to 210/110 while working and I went to the ER multiple times with heart attack symptoms. I didn't have the big one, but I had markers for small heart attacks. The only way to stave off heart attack symptoms was to run 10 to 12 miles a day, every day. My heart rate was 130 at rest. They had me on 5 different heart meds and nothing relieved the need for me to run 10 miles a day. Then I got the adrenal cancer test result, which was negative. Then I woke up with a new symptom.

I awoke with a bleeding, blistering rash on my arms. I was diagnosed with a drug eruption rash from my beta blocker. I had to come off cold turkey as I was at risk of my skin sheeting off the greater percentage of my body. That sent me back to the ER with another minor heart attack.

The rash eventually cleared, but I was getting weaker and weaker. Then my back gave out again and I no longer had the ability to run off the excess adrenaline. I was terrified. Luckily my doctor figured out the heart/blood pressure issue, it was rare but treatable. For some reason, I continued to crumble. Work was stressful, my marriage was falling apart. I felt like a failure. I was losing everything. I had bought more home than I could afford. I was just trying to hold it together till Allie got her first job after graduation. That was the plan. Allie had just graduated and promised that she would help bail us out. She didn't find a job for a year and when she did, her money was just that, hers. I was a "loser that should be able to take better care of his family." I once again contemplated ending my life as it crumbled around me. I had no refuge. Not at work, not at home. No close true friends nearby. I could only see one way out.

~ *The Garage* ~

I felt worthless. It was almost like imposter syndrome. On the outside, I had a successful career, the big house with a pool, the sports car, the designer dogs, a full pro shop in my garage. It was everything that I had ever dreamed of having and I was miserable. We were miserable. I began googling things. One of Allie's main fears/complaints was that I would die, and she and the kids would be out on the street because I only had life insurance through work. I explained that I had over 800k in life insurance through work and that if something happened to me, they would be okay.

Her reply to that was, "you won't die quick Stoney, you'll drag it out until your work benefits expire. You are too much of a fighter. We won't get any of that money." That is why I was googling things, things like, how long do you have to have life insurance before they will pay a benefit because of suicide. Some sites said one year, some said two years, I had been at my job for nearly three years. I should be covered. One day, when everyone had gone to school and work except for me, I wrote a note, a suicide note. I apologized for being sick, for not being strong enough, for failing to take care of them and gave my last words of advice to my children. I folded the note and placed it under a vase on the kitchen Island. I wrote a second note that I taped to the inside of the door leading to the garage. My kids might beat Allie home. The note was short. "Please don't open this door. Call your mom. I love you and I am so sorry. Dad"

I grabbed the gun out of the closet and stood in the garage with it pressed against my temple. My only fear was that I would flinch and live. There were three mirrors in the garage, and I stared at myself with a gun to my head, then in my mouth. I tasted the cold metal of that Sig Saur on my tongue. It was cold, yet welcoming. Simultaneous tears of anger and despair ran down my face. The despair of not feeling like there was a way out and the anger that I was stalling, that I wasn't even strong enough to pull the trigger. I was scheduled to work in an hour, and I stared into my own broken eyes, gun against my head, applying tension against the trigger, just attempting to summon the will, to end it all.

I dropped the gun down, walked back into the house and shredded the notes, placed the gun back in the closet and headed to work. Feeling more distraught than ever and an odd disgust for myself for not being strong enough to end it all. I lost count of how many suicide notes that I shredded over a two-month period. Each time I felt like a failure both when I would write the notes and then equally or even more so, when I would shred them.

~ All at Once ~

I worked long hours. I picked up extra shifts, hell I picked up an extra job trying to keep us afloat. I had a three day stretch of 18-hour days where I forgot to drink water. I collapsed in the parking lot one night while walking to my car. It felt like Guillain Barre. I was terrified as I was being taken to the hospital. I didn't have a partner to lean on, Allie had told me for the past 2 years that all we were was roommates. Then the doctor told me what I already knew.

"You are dead in six months." It doesn't get more real than that. He told me that I should not be able to do the things that I am doing and that my time was running out unless I changed jobs. I told him that I couldn't afford to take a pay cut; he asked who would take care of my kids if I was dead. I knew Allie couldn't do it. So, I began looking for another job and put our giant house on the market. I got a job offer, my house sold, and my father died on the same day. It was fate, but with a catch.

The catch was that it was a $30k decrease in pay. I was bankrupt the moment that I pulled my license off the wall of the job that was killing me. I told Allie, she wasn't happy, but said she wouldn't tell me whether I could quit or not. She said, "if you get even sicker, you'll blame me for it." I spread my father's ashes. He worked so hard his whole life. He missed my childhood. The next day, I bankrupted myself to see my children grow up. I bankrupted myself to extend my life.

~ Moving to DFW ~

I accepted the position in DFW. I was up against 106 other applicants. It had to be fate; it had to put me where I was supposed to be. I had some life insurance money from my father and that allowed us to make the move and have a decent Christmas for the kids. Allie was taking this well, or so I thought.

When the money ran out, it really set in with her that life was going to change. I loved my new position, but my take home pay was a thousand less every 2 weeks and I was barely hanging on financially. I was better health-wise though, much better. It was now 2020 and as we know that is when everything started to change. I called it in February, I told my staff to brace themselves for the worst years of their careers. I braced myself too, COVID was coming, and I was standing in a pharmacy with 4 autoimmune diseases and only 25k in life insurance with an unemployed wife.

It was the first week of March. The hysteria hadn't set in yet. Nobody really thought that COVID was going to be that big of a deal, except for me. Maybe it was because I had so much to lose. Maybe it was because I was the guy that was supposed to die from it. It ran through my mind constantly. We weren't to the point of mandatory masks yet. I was at work, and I heard yelling from the drop off window of my pharmacy.

~ *The Ten Dollar Cough* ~

An elderly woman was irate that her cough medicine wasn't covered by Medicare. It is against Medicare law for cough meds to be covered as they can increase chances of complications like pneumonia as well as having other deleterious effects on the elderly population. I explained this to her in a calm and empathetic fashion, I am good with people. I put a coupon on her script and got it down to $10. How did she thank me? She coughed right in my face on purpose, twice!

I was dumbfounded. I was at a loss for words. Her script had "possible COVID" written across the top by her doctor. If she had COVID, it could kill me. My kids and wife would be homeless within months. They were not testing people who hadn't traveled or been in contact with a confirmed case. All I could do was wait and see. I would know in a week or so.

~ *A COVID Split* ~

I went downhill on day 5. I had trouble breathing. I coughed incessantly. I could barely walk across my living room. I had COVID. I gasped for air. I couldn't think straight. I didn't know if I would make it. My pulse ox started dropping into the low 90s. Then I got handed something that I wasn't expecting. Divorce papers, when I was at my lowest, my sickest. I got handed divorce papers.

Allie told me that I could cohabitate with her and the kids, but we were nothing more than roommates as I had ruined her life. We would have to live in an apartment or rent for 5 years until my credit recovered and that was too much of a sacrifice for her. She was resentful and angry that I had destroyed us financially and I wouldn't be allowed to take her down with me. She said I wasn't even a man anymore, that I failed to protect my family. She said the papers were "standard and fair." Through teary, COVID glazed eyes, I just signed the papers without even reading them. I was broken and didn't really think I could beat COVID anyway, what did it matter?

It would be a month before I would test negative and be strong enough to go back to work in the pharmacy. The verbal berating went on daily while I was home. I was perhaps the lowest that I had ever been. I looked at Misty's Facebook profile that month. She looked so happy. She was more beautiful than ever. She was successful. She had it all together. I wanted to message her and tell her that I didn't blame her for me fighting with mom. I wanted to relieve her of that weight, if she had carried it around all these years. I just couldn't though. I couldn't be like that deadbeat dad that was gone for all those years that shows up dying wanting attention and comfort. She didn't deserve that sort of stress. She didn't need to see me like this. I didn't want her to see me like this. But God, I just wanted to hear her voice one more time. She appeared happily married, out of respect for that, I didn't reach out. It was now time to stand in a pharmacy again.

~ *The Attack* ~

By the time I went back to work in April, the hysteria of COVID was in full swing. I was incredibly fatigued. Still gasping for air. I had what would later be called Long COVID. I got through the days though. My team was paranoid for me. They protected me as best they could. They shielded me from patients that were coughing and made sure that I always had access to food and water. It was the best work family that I had ever had. I was so tired that I literally stumbled and fell in the pharmacy. My techs had tears in their eyes when I would pick myself up off the floor and get back to work. I tried to start jogging again one morning to open my lungs. I blacked out and fell across a curb. I walked home and got ready for work. When I got home, I had the worst headache of my life. Allie gasped when she looked at me and told me to look in the mirror.

One side of my face was drooping. I drove myself to the ER. I didn't even ask her to drive me, after all we were just roommates now. Truthfully, I didn't want her to drive me. The diagnosis was transient ischemic attack, a mini stroke. That was why I blacked out. I may have even had two. This was now a known Long COVID risk.

I was transported to another hospital in Dallas via ambulance. Upon arrival I was asked if anyone at my place of employment had been diagnosed with COVID. I worked at Sam's, of course there were people that had tested positive, but they didn't have contact with me. That didn't matter. Without me knowing what was happening, suddenly, I was being wheeled onto the COVID floor. I was surrounded by healthcare professionals in Hazmat suits, communicating through glass windows and terrified out of my mind that I was going to contract COVID a second time. I could hear the coughs, gasps and coding of patients in the adjacent rooms. This went on for days before I was allowed to be discharged. I once again returned to work.

A couple of weeks went by and then another set of symptoms started.

~ *Rash Decisions* ~

I developed something that looked like the Lupus rash. My fatigue worsened. My coordination worsened and I started to get a bleeding rash. They pulled countless vials of blood out of me to try and figure it out. On the top of the list once again, cancer. This time, blood cancer.

If I worked late, I was in the doctor's office early and vice versa for months. It took them 2 months to completely rule out cancer. Nothing fits. Nothing made sense until I woke up one morning to find my sheets spattered with blood.

Allie and I have now slept in different rooms for months, so I made the discovery on my own. I had developed so many blood blisters across my back, arms and legs that they were coalescing and bursting when I laid on them. I would go to work, and the blood would seep through my slacks and my shirt. My techs just stared at this man who was falling apart in front of their very eyes. I once again went to the ER. I presented with multiple types of rashes all at once. The doctor blasted me with steroids but told me that they had no idea what was going on. I got referred to a dermatologist and luckily got in within 2 days. This woman told me what every man longs to hear.

She asked me to remove my clothes, I did so and then she said it. "Wow, this is cool! Can I get more people in here?" Not the circumstance in which you want to hear those words, but still I can truthfully say that I have had that exchange with a woman. Soon, I had other doctors, students and nurses examining me, the unicorn. The diagnosis, dermatomyositis. A disease that affects only 1 in 200,000 people. It attacks and destroys the muscle and skin. The therapy takes months to kick in, if it does at all. The other risk factor is cancer, 30-40% risk within 3 years. The treatment? Massive immunosuppression for a frontline healthcare worker during a pandemic. What could go wrong there?

I took a leave of absence from work to start therapy, as the risk of me standing in a pharmacy being severely immunosuppressed was simply too great. The more time that I spent at home, the more a theory that Allie and I had kicked around started to make sense. Hancock.

~ *An Unexpected Call* ~

My phone rang one evening as I struggled walking around the block. My godson, my best friend's son, called me. In a cool panic, if there is such a thing. He had tried and begged to no avail, as had his sister, to accomplish something. He asked me to save his dad. I was confused. You see, my best friend and I had one of those relationships that stood the test of time, but life put us hundreds of miles apart and we'd go months at a time without speaking, but still we were still 'close' to each other. My godson felt that I was the only one that could talk sense into his dad. He asked if I was healthy enough to come up to see him. I said that I'd find a way.

I called Chris the next day. I opened with "what's up champ?' He laughed a sad laugh. And said "huh champ? I hadn't felt like that in a while." Little did I know that my godson was with him. He was sitting on the floor of his closet crying. I'd only seen him cry twice. My mother's funeral and his sister's funeral. He was broken. Few things in life can break you like a mate can...especially when they are supposed to be your soulmate.

I could hear his son again pleading with him to choose his children over his soulmate, but he couldn't. His son had filled me in a bit, but not nearly all of it, but enough to know that for the first time in my life that soulmate had now somehow become a more fluid terminology. I am a wordsmith, and I was scrambling, but hit him as hard as I could through the phone. I said, "brother, you're confusing familiarity with functionality." I could hear the pain through the silence. We spoke a bit more, but I could tell that I had fragmented him. I had to do it. I had to find a way to get to him. I offered to drive to OKC to have lunch and talk with him. I made a promise to his son to save him from himself, but it was more than that. I had to save my best friend, the closest thing to a brother that I had ever known and will ever know again. He agreed to lunch, just him and I.

I even made a post on Facebook about it to lock him into the bro date. I made it to the Red River, and he texted me a question. "Is it okay if Kelly comes?" I screamed fuck in my car! She knew. She knew that he could still be reached...if he was away from her. I was too sick to waste the trip. It would accomplish nothing. So, I risked it. I said no. It had to be just us two and no one else. I waited for the reply. I kept driving north, praying that he still had the spine that he used to possess. He did not. He said, sorry I must cancel then. I deleted the Facebook post, turned back south and headed home.

~ *Fight Night* ~

I made a promise to his son, and I was bound and determined to fulfill that promise. I brainstormed as I walked around the block each night. Who knew that Mike Tyson would be the catalyst that I needed? Iron Mike to the rescue!

There were rumblings and excitement about a Mike Tyson fight with Roy Jones Jr. It was a pay per view event. I called Chris on the day of the fight. I asked if he was going to watch the fight. He almost ashamedly admitted that he had bought the fight. I asked if he wanted to watch the fight together, remember we were four hours apart. He said, "how are we going to do that?" I said, "I am already driving north brother." He exclaimed, "really?!" He was stoked and I was on a mission!

He stopped and got liquor and snacks on the way home from work and I kept driving north.   At this time, I had already downsized to an apartment and when I pulled into his driveway, his home looked like a castle. He opened the door and hugged me, one of those, it's been too long hugs. He was tiny. I was heavy, yes, but he was small. A shell, a fit shell, but certainly not the Chris that I remembered. We made our way through to his entertainment room, yes, he had an entertainment room. He appeared to be doing well for himself, keyword, appeared.

We watched the undercard bouts and talked a bit, but not much. We had the French doors shut, but Kelly would pop in from time to time, almost like surveillance. The whole room would shift when she entered. She knew I was sick; she offered medical advice with wild eyes that wanted to be understood, eyes that I am sure, longed for the understanding of herself when she'd look in the mirror. She wasn't the Kelly that I remembered. Not even close. I humored her, while dissecting her, but said nothing. She left the room and Chris leaned over, tapped me on the shoulder and asked me a question. "It's not just me, right? She is batshit crazy right?" I said, without hesitation, "100% she is coocoo for coco puffs bro."

I honestly can't remember much of the fights, but I can remember seeing my best friend fragmented and his wife utterly shattered. Chris was aware of his fragmentation. Kelly on the other hand was seemingly euphoric in her delusional bliss. I did my best to set the foundation for change. I spent the night and part of the next day, reassuring Chris that it was indeed not him, but instead her, that had an altered grip on reality. I tried, but knew that I needed more time, but I didn't have it. I drove back south to Texas praying that I had indeed given him some sort of clarity. I went home to conduct an experiment.

~ *Hancock Experiment* ~

If you are unfamiliar with the movie Hancock, watch it, as this is a spoiler alert. You have two immortals that are forces for good. They are drawn to each other. However, the issue is that the closer they become to each other, the more and more mortal they become. I was never sick as a child. I wanted to be sick. I played sick from the second day of kindergarten, just to miss school. The only time that I was sick before Allie was when I was 19 and I was with Misty. I got chicken pox at 19 and it leveled me for weeks. After that, however, I was invincible for years until I dated Allie. Pneumonia, flu, ulcers, Guillain Barre, Celiac Disease, Raynaud's, Psoriasis, Dermatomyositis just to name a few. It even got to the point that if we were getting along and cuddled or had sex, I was sicker and weaker the next day. We talked about it one night. She asked if I thought she literally made me ill. There was only one way to find out. I would spend time with someone else and see how I felt. We agreed to the experiment as I had been demoted to "just a fucking roommate" for the past year. Her words, not mine.

Enter my first "date" in 17 years. She was kind, completely unlike anyone I had ever been on a date with before, but kind. We had a good dinner and talked for a bit. I walked away from that date feeling better. Then I went on another date with her, then another. The more time I spent away from Allie, the better I felt. It was obvious enough that it hurt and angered Allie. Honestly, I thought it was hilarious. A real-life succubus. Wow, who would have thought.

This woman was coarse but had a sense of humor. She was kind, a bit wild and could cook. I had to have four back procedures in as many weeks, and she showed genuine care. She acted like she gave a damn. Surgeries were risky for me with the history of Guillain Barre. I could wake up paralyzed again, I could relapse weeks later, or I could go into cardiovascular collapse. I signed the waiver and agreed to the surgery as I had put off repairing my back because of these fears for years. They wheeled me to the operating room.

~ *Anesthesia Goggles* ~

I looked around the room and was trying to stay calm. All those memories of Guillain Barre came flooding back. They let me know that they were starting the anesthesia. I immediately started having complications from the anesthesia and nearly went into cardiovascular collapse as I went under. I could hear my vitals being read aloud as I was supposed to go to sleep. I fought the anesthesia for 4 minutes, terrified as I heard my heart rate and blood pressures swing wildly. The anesthesiologist came around to my face and said, "I swear to God, I will bring you back. Just let go and relax." I felt tears rolling down my face as I drifted off thinking of my children.

When I opened my eyes, I saw my anesthesiologist. He patted me on the shoulder and said, "I told you that I would bring you back." I came out of anesthesia rough as well. I was beyond panicked, and I felt drunk. I texted the woman that I had started dating that I loved her.

I didn't love her, she knew that, and I knew that, but I texted it. It was out there now, and Allie looked through my phone and saw the text. It hurt her. She said that she felt betrayed and hurt. She didn't want me, but she didn't want me to be happy with someone else either. She was pissed that I felt physically better when I wasn't around her. Proof of how negatively she impacted my health because of how toxic our relationship had become over the years. Then, I started coughing. It couldn't be, could it?

~ *The Duffle Bag* ~

I went to get tested. I was coughing a little bit, but mostly it was a sore throat. I wasn't expecting a positive result. I sat and waited in that downtown Dallas urgent care clinic. When the doctor came back into the room, he stood in the corner. Fuck, I was positive. He confirmed it. The date itself stood out to me; it was the 22nd anniversary of my mother being laid to rest. I texted Allie and let her know to clear a path to my bedroom so I wouldn't be in contact with anyone. I texted the lady I went on dates with and let her know that she needed to be tested as well. As I pulled in the driveway, Allie called my phone. I answered and was baffled by what she had to say.

"You aren't allowed in the house. You've got a duffle bag with your meds and a couple of days of clothes inside it. Go, stay with the woman that you told her that you loved. You can't come home again." I was at a loss for words. I texted Joanne what had just happened, she did not offer me a place to stay. I didn't ask directly. I was immunocompromised, I had covid again and I had three grand in my pocket. I had nowhere and no means to quarantine for 14 days.

When Allie had an affair, I fought for her. I fought for our family. I swallowed my pride. I could be dying and the woman that I raised a family with for the last 17 years just said best of luck and go fuck yourself. I was homeless. I went to the gas station in Keller, Texas and filled the gas tank. I could feel my breathing getting more and more labored. I was coughing more by the minute. I was weaker by the second. I had a wonderful, awful idea of where I wanted to go. Vegas baby! I started driving west at 4pm.

~ *Woes and Backroads* ~

There was no going back. There was no chance for marital healing. It was truly over, forever. I didn't cry. Not a single tear. She had truly shown that she didn't believe that I was worth fighting for anymore. In fact, she had never fought for me, and she never would.

I had wanted to go to Vegas for years. I wanted to see the lights one more time. I truly felt that I wasn't going to survive COVID again, there was no way, not with as weak as I was from battling dermatomyositis. After an hour of driving, I could feel myself burning up with a fever. I posted on Facebook that I was COVID positive again and left it at that. I didn't want anyone to know that I had just been thrown out of my home, for that matter, thrown out of my life.

The miles were a blur. I ended up on back highways trying to get to the panhandle of Texas. If I could just manage to get there, then it was a straight shot west on I-40 for 800 miles to get to Vegas. I was coughing so hard that my vision was blurring, and it felt like I was drifting in and out of consciousness, much like I am certain that I was drifting in and out of my lane. My best friend Chris called me to check on me. He wasn't even on Facebook that day. He said that he just had a feeling that he needed to call me. I told him that I was kicked out of my home and about my plan to see the lights of Vegas before I got too sick. He lost his mind. He begged me to come to his home in Oklahoma. I refused and told him that I loved him and continued my drive west. Within another 2 hours I felt like I wasn't going to make it to Vegas. I was crumbling faster and faster. I'd die somewhere in New Mexico or Arizona. It was now 11pm and I was in the middle of nowhere gasping worse and worse. Chris kept calling and texting. I answered, my replies were bookended with coughing and gagging.

I could hear the panic in his voice as I tried and failed to talk without coughing. He asked me where I was, and I really didn't know for sure. I said somewhere in west Texas. I googled his address to get directions, I was over 5 hours away from him, there was no way on earth that I could make it to him. I got a room and promised to head his way after I got some sleep.

~ Brother Bound ~

Somehow, I made it to Amarillo. This was at the height of COVID. I was supposed to be quarantined but had no choice. It was cold outside, so the redness of my fever was coverable due to the freezing temps in Amarillo. I checked in, feeling guilty for any contact that I had with an unsuspecting person. Hoping and praying that I didn't kill someone or someone that they loved. Stifling coughs and shaking so badly that I could barely get my credit card out of my wallet, I secured my room for the night. I didn't even change clothes, I simply collapsed on the bed and passed out unsure if I'd even make it through the night.

Come morning I was sweating so badly on the way to Chris's house that my jeans were soaked within an hour of my departure. I was more tired than I had been since my battle with Guillain Barre. I was nodding off at the wheel, coughing more and even more short of breath. The drive seemed like it was 15 hours instead of 3. The drive was a blur. I remember driving past my old college. What a beacon of hope that institution was for us. Us? That was a weird thought now. There was no us, not anymore. I fought so hard for the piece of paper. To have it framed and placed on a wall in a pharmacy to prove that I knew what I was doing. A symbolic display that I had learned all about medicine, the human body, that I knew how to help people stay "here." Fast forward to now and my hope was to perish quickly enough that my employer paid life insurance would still be in effect. When I arrived, Chris met me in the driveway, I collapsed into his arms, and he helped me into his home.

~ *The Ironic Safe Harbor* ~

I strained to get out the words I am sorry and thank you...His reply? "It was never a question." That was my best friend's response when he brought me into his home with his family while being COVID positive. Between coughs, I told him that he was risking himself and his family. His reply, "you ARE my family." He led me to his movie room where he and his family had made up the couch and a recliner for me. The same room where I had shown up to save him was now my very own "safe harbor." One of the things that I always admired was his calmness. He never really seemed emotional or rattled, ever. When I collapsed into the recliner, gasping and coughing, I looked at him and I saw something I hadn't seen before, fear. I hadn't looked in a mirror for 36 hours, now I didn't have to, his look of fear told me everything that I needed to know. He looked at me and said with an oddly stern, yet shaky voice, "this is not how you end."

I wasn't the only one who was struggling that year. Chris was coming off the worst year of his life as well, in fact, he was still battling it. His marriage of 25 years was now laying in shambles. Shambles that anyone but him could recognize, that they could never be molded back together. Still, he welcomed me in, to give me shelter during my storm even if it meant me seeing him at his weakest, at his worst, at his most vulnerable. He had lost his marriage and the fear in his eyes stemmed from the possibility of witnessing first-hand the loss of his best friend.

Between gasps and coughs, I gave him and his wife, yes, she still lived in the home, specific instructions to treat me as a hazardous substance and to keep their distance. The TV room had French doors which would remain shut except for the exchange of food and Gatorade. I was still so worried that I would get them all sick. The amount of guilt that I felt while I shook and sweated in that recliner the first night, was palpable. They went to the pharmacy to get me a pulse ox and a blood pressure cuff, so I could keep track of the rate of my demise. My pulse ox dipped from my starting point of 99 to 96 the first night at his home. I shook and gasped and coughed most of the night, I jerked awake when my phone rang bright and early the next morning.

~ *Social Butterfly Takes Flight* ~

I looked at the phone and it was Joanne. Remember her? The woman that I professed my love to while coming out of anesthesia? She must be calling to check on me, as she said she loved me too. She must feel bad for not offering me a place to stay. It turns out, not so much. Me being sick was not going to work for her. She explained she was a "social butterfly" and that me having to hide away during a pandemic would just cause more problems for us later. Day 3 of COVID she broke up with me as Chris walked into the COVID wing of his home to check on me. I hung up the phone and laughed and coughed and coughed and laughed. He knew something was up. I explained the situation and he just shook his head as I appeared happy over the last couple weeks as I dated her. I joked and said, "it is fine, I'm fine. My world is on fire, but it's all good." Chris was now my only kind adult interaction on the planet. That was okay, I had my hands full fighting COVID anyway. My pulse ox had now dipped to 93. He offered me a means of distraction while he went to work all day. He could see it. Winter was coming!

~ Winter is Coming ~

I was still getting weaker and weaker. I have been ultra-rare in terms of my health status; in fact, I am 1 in 200 billion. I also learned that I was the rare person that had not seen the Game of Thrones. This would be my distraction. Chris inserted disk one and left for work. I am not usually a fan of that genre of entertainment, but alcoholism, violence, copious sex scenes and dragons, I will have to admit is quite captivating. As entertained as I was, I was now facing a new challenge just hours later.

It came time to change to the next disc of GOT. I stood up out of my recliner, took a step toward the tv and fell between the couch and the coffee table. I didn't have the strength to move for what seemed like an eternity. I managed to crawl to the blue ray player and change the disc. It was six feet, but it took me 20 minutes to cover that paltry splay of carpet to climb back into my recliner. My pulse ox was now 92. I looked at my clothes and I was now bleeding through them in a few spots.

Not from the fall per-se, but my dermatomyositis was now flaring quite a bit due to my COVID. While trying to process the blood spots, my phone rang, and I answered it coughing and out of breath.

~ No More Talking ~

Once I stopped coughing and gasping, I heard the voices of my children on the other end of the phone. I was so happy to hear their voices. They were what was keeping me alive, they were the reason that I was fighting to stay alive. Much like when I was fighting through ICU with Guillain Barre, they were my focus. I tried desperately to hide the sounds of my gasping and coughing. They asked how I was doing, and I told them that it was rough, but I was going to beat it. My daughter said, "of course you are because you're unkillable." It made me grin, as she'd been calling me unkillable for about a year. Every time that I would face a stroke, a heart attack or a new autoimmune disease in the past year or so she'd tell me she wasn't worried. She wasn't worried because she and her brother thought of me as unkillable. They told me that they loved me and to keep fighting as we ended our call. I received a text message from my ex an hour later telling me that I wasn't allowed to talk to them on the phone until I had beaten COVID. I was told that I sounded so bad that they cried when they hung up the phone. I was only allowed to text my kids from that point forward. My heart sank at the idea that it could have been the last time that I heard my children's voices. My neck went limp, and I looked down at my shirt and I saw fresh blood seeping through my chest.

~ Laundry ~

I had been taking immunosuppressive meds to control my dermatomyositis prior to getting COVID a second time. Upon diagnosis, I was well controlled, and I agreed with my doc when he made the decision to stop my meds when I got COVID. We just didn't have enough data at that point and if I got secondary pneumonia, I might not be able to fight it off.

When I climbed back into the recliner after my crawl back from the blue ray player, evidently, I had developed large blood-filled blisters on my torso that popped under the pressure of the friction caused by pulling myself into the recliner. I looked under my shirt and I had several blood blisters the size of half dollars that were oozing blood because I tore them open. I couldn't treat the disease because it would let COVID run through me completely unchecked. By morning I had painful bleeding lesions on my back, buttocks, arms and legs and there was nothing I could do to stop it without risking further complications from COVID. Chris came in as I looked at my duffle bag of dirty clothes and asked if I needed laundry done. I told him that I would get my own laundry done and tried to stand, but fell to my knees immediately, breaking more blisters open to weep blood. For the last 17 years, I was the one who did the laundry and the dishes in my home, no matter how sick I was. Tears streamed down my face as I ashamedly let him wash my clothes so I could get out of my blood-soaked clothes later that night. I was broken and I was helpless.

Day 6 had me rebounding. I awoke with a pulse ox of 96. I was breathing a bit easier, and my cough was improving as well. I knew this was coming. I had already done a great deal of research since I was immuno-suppressed. This is the moment of truth. I had either beaten it and was getting out of the proverbial woods or the second wave would hit around days 9, 10 or 11. That is when the people who are going to succumb to COVID go back downhill. My oxygen transfer was so much better that I could walk to the bathroom and trim my beard. I didn't have to crawl to the Blu-ray player for the next installment of sex and dragons, I mean the Game of Thrones. The next few days afforded me some cautious optimism. Then day 10 hit.

~ *Grey Anatomy* ~

The morning of day 10 I awoke with my clothes drenched in sweat and burning up with a fever. I was gasping again and fumbled for my pulse ox. I had tumbled down to 91. I was having so much more trouble moving air. I was so lightheaded that I felt drunk. The days were blurring together. I couldn't even keep track of the time of day either. Drifting in and out of consciousness all day. Crawling to the bathroom to vomit no matter how much Zofran I had dosed myself with. At the end of day 10 Chris checked on me when he got home. My eyes were closed, I was ashen, and my chest wasn't moving hardly at all. He held his breath as he checked my pulse not knowing whether or not it would be there. It was still there. He let me sleep and shut the door.

Day 11 went much the same way. I started the day with a pulse ox of 90. I could feel stuff settling in my lungs. It scared me as it reminded me of the sludge that I felt in my lungs in the ICU when I battled Guillain Barre. I tried googling the urgent care close by to be evaluated but kept getting lightheaded and passing out before dialing the number multiple times. I felt markedly worse than the day before. Once again Chris came in to check on me when he got home from work. I was more ashen and this time my chest was not moving at all. He made his way to me and checked my pulse and had trouble finding it. He pressed on my chest, and I awoke gasping for air. He would later tell me that he thought he had found his best friend dead in a recliner two days in a row. I got to the urgent care and was diagnosed with pneumonia in my left lung. The treatment was complicated. I couldn't go with the treatment of choice, as it was too dangerous because of a drug interaction with the immunosuppressive med that was still in my system. It could cause an arrythmia and/or sudden death. So, we went with doxycycline instead of azithromycin since my body was under so much stress that my resting pulse was already at 130 beats per minute. I was brittle, my eyes rolling into the back of my head while trying to talk to Chris. I passed out in a pool of sweat not knowing if I could beat this thing or not. Chris was afraid that I wouldn't make it much longer too, he messaged Misty, my first wife, to let her know I was with him and battling COVID.

Day 12 began with Chris sitting in the other recliner and telling me that he messaged Misty to let her know what was going on with me. I hated that. I didn't want her to think of me in this way, weak, helpless and homeless if not for the charity of my best friend. I thought of her daily from that moment forward. Would I be in the same spot if I had been with her. I hoped not as I never wanted her to see me like this. I remembered when I got chicken pox when I was nineteen. I looked like a lizard and didn't want her to see me, but she wouldn't stay away. I looked monstrous when she saw me. Did she flinch? Not for a second. I'll never forget how she painfully said, "baby" and then held my pox covered face and kissed me like she still saw the man that lay underneath my battered skin. I was glad I didn't have to hear the pain in her voice that would certainly be there if she saw everything that I had been going through the last few years.

~ Just a Bit Tachy ~

On days 13 and 14 I spiraled down quicker and farther. By the end of day 14 my pulse ox dipped to 87. I could barely breathe. Every time up to this point in my life, I could see the other side of the struggle. I could see me beating it, no matter what it was that I was fighting. This was different. I couldn't see the other side of this one. That shook me to my core. I went to the hospital when I developed chest pain. I got put on oxygen upon arrival. They started doing x-rays on my lungs. I had scarring on both lungs and was diagnosed with double pneumonia. The doxycycline wasn't working, I was switched to the more effective, yet infinitely more dangerous option of azithromycin. Once my breathing stabilized that night, I was sent home to minimize my exposure to other opportunistic infections due to being immunosuppressed. The next morning, I would start the antibiotic and hope that my heart would tolerate it.

I took the first dose, 2 tablets of azithromycin in the morning knowing that I really had no other choice as I had to treat the pneumonia to stay out of the hospital. By late afternoon my resting heart rate was 140 beats per minute. If I could tolerate it through the night, I would have a chance since the next 4 days had dosing of only one tablet per day. That night by 11pm my chest was hurting terribly, and my resting heart rate was now at 150. I was in a dead sweat and had the uncontrollable urge to move my legs. It felt like adrenaline was surging through my body. I just knew that I wasn't going to make it. My chest felt like it was in a vise. I took nitroglycerin like they were tic-tacs to trade the chest pain for headaches for the next few hours. I couldn't imagine myself being alive in the morning.

This would continue for the next 5 days while I finished the antibiotic therapy. My heart rate raced like I was sprinting even though I was nearly sedentary. By day twenty my pulse ox rebounded to 96 again and I now had the strength to walk to the kitchen. It was surreal to feel so accomplished by being able to walk to the next room. This too brought back memories of Guillain Barre that I had never wanted to revisit. It was like graduating from that apartment in the skilled rehabilitation facility.

~ *Sunlight and the Gremlin* ~

I had the urge to move beyond the confines of my best friend's home. I wanted to go outside. I wanted to walk, I desperately wanted to walk. I needed to know "where" I was at in terms of my physical state. Even if it was awful, I needed a starting point, a distance to beat the second time and every time after that. It was how I started my journey back after Guillain Barre and somehow this felt eerily similar. At the height of my recovery from Guillain Barre, I was running at least 6 miles every single morning. I made my way outside and immediately turned back inside from the pain. Not in my legs, but my skin. My dermatomyositis and nerve damage had gotten so bad that it felt like I had scalding water poured on my arms when the sunlight hit them. I was officially a gremlin. I needed long sleeves and sunscreen when it was the day after Christmas and 50 degrees. I put those on and headed back outside. The best way that I can describe it is that it was like having a severe sunburn and then going back outside the next day. I could still feel the heat and sting through heavy clothing, hell I could feel it through my jeans. It was still uncomfortable, but tolerable. I made it about 100 feet before I started swaying with exhaustion. I stumbled back inside and collapsed in my recliner in exhaustion. I'd try again the next day.

Day after day, I covered up like a beekeeper and trudged down the street. Further and further each day, even if it was just a foot or two, if it was further, it gave me some sense of accomplishment. I was still struggling to breathe each day, but I ventured further none-the-less. I was still recovering from pneumonia. I started using my albuterol inhaler and took nitroglycerin with me on my outings as I constantly felt like I was having a heart attack even when I was just walking briskly. Then on January 1st, a breakthrough, I jogged a quarter of a mile, it was slow, but it instilled within me some hope. I collapsed in the doorway of my bedroom and fell asleep on the floor. I woke up six hours later. I could indeed move more now, but it devastated me. The next morning, I limped into the kitchen and Chris was there.

~ A Brother in Arms ~

Chris asked if he could jog with me that morning. He had a look of worry on his face. I had told him about my bedroom floor nap from the day before. I was still fighting so hard to lift my feet to jog, still pounding albuterol and nitro just to get through it. I told him that it wasn't pretty. I told him that it would be hard to watch. I told him that I had to get to a different "place" to do what I was doing. He promised not to judge and that he just wanted to be there if I needed him. You see he had raced across the kitchen a mere week ago to catch me as I swayed and started to fall to the floor. Again, he was afraid of losing his best friend. I was ashamed of how weak that I was, so brittle and frankly so scared. He always told me that I was the strongest person he'd ever known, and I didn't want him to see me struggle so badly while attempting to rebuild myself. He wouldn't take no for an answer.

We started out and adrenaline carried me half a mile and then I shut down. He stayed behind me and patted me on the back. I was dying on the inside and walked for a couple minutes and started back up. I made it another quarter mile and snuck a nitro to ease the chest pain, and I swayed when the dizziness hit me. It was the farthest that I had been so far. I was trying and failing to hide the gasping. I rolled my head toward Chris, and he waited for my lead. He was afraid to push me harder. I nodded my head and tried to start running again, I was flailing and angry at myself, yelling in frustration, yelling because of how weak I felt. He yelled, with me and at me, to push because he knew me, he knew I wasn't ready to quit. I ran harder and started to lose my footing and collapsed onto him. He put my arm over his shoulder and once again carried the burden of his best friend, who once again could not carry his own weight. I kept going and going. Out of ego, embarrassment, pride, rage, fear and everything else that I could muster. Stops and starts, screams of agony. Screams of frustration. I got close to home and I broke down in tears. He once again told me that I was the strongest man he had ever known. I said, "really? I can barely walk right now." His teary eyes looked into mine and he replied, "You are REALLY the strongest man I've ever known. You shouldn't be alive, and you just jogged/walked 5.17 miles." That run was important, he pointed out something that I couldn't see through the pain in my joints, my chest and my aching lungs. He told me that I still had more fight in me than I had realized.

The road back would be arduous. Not as dramatic this time, no paralysis, but no guarantee of a steady recovery either. I was disabled for the second time in a year because of Covid/Dermatomyositis. Chris had moved me into the in-law portion of his home. This was where his daughter Aaliyah had been situated. I felt guilty, but he assured me that she liked the idea of moving into the main area of the house. It was separated from the main house by a long hallway and had its own entrance. I had lived there for a month and had barely seen his daughter. I met her a few times when she was younger, but for all intents and purposes a stranger had moved into her house. A friend of her father's, but an unknown to her. A man struggling to breathe, stumbling and falling, bleeding through his clothes. I could feel the awkwardness and I hated that.

The move to the other end of the house had its perks though. It gave me a bathroom that connected two bedrooms in a jack and jill layout. This way, my kids would have a place to stay in our own little space when I was well enough to have visitors. I went the longest that I have ever gone without seeing my kids. I went for 21 days, then saw them for a couple days after Christmas. I was weaker than the last time that I saw them, when I picked up that duffle bag off our porch in early December. They were somewhat used to seeing me weak, but this was the worst it'd been in a while. It was the weakest my son could recall seeing me for sure. He was too small to remember my battle with Guillain Barre.

~ *Resolutions* ~

There is a saying that people are too busy working to make any real money. I believe that to be true, but there is something about solitude as well. There is something about being captive in a room. There is something about disability. There is something about wrestling with your own mortality. It makes you think. It gives you clarity. It gives you a new perspective. That you are too busy to achieve during a normal existence to comprehend the gravity of the daily decisions that can weigh you down without even perceiving weight of it. Before you know it, you're drowning in a reality that should not be your own. Drowning without even trying to save yourself. Taking on water and mistaking it for air with every gasp.

I wasn't the same man, that collapsed into my friend's arms back in December. That solitude changed me. For years, I went to war at work and then went to war at home. I had a cave to fight out of now. No fighting, no distractions, no walking on eggshells, all that I had on my plate was just getting better. I was weak, but somehow, I knew that when she gave me that duffle bag, she gave me a gift. The gift of time, and that time afforded me reflection. I needed that desperately. I never really made New Year's Resolutions, but that year...I made 41.

1. Embrace my creative talents

2.Finish writing my book

3. Train like Rocky

4. Have the Confidence of Apollo Creed

5. Survive Like Rocky

6. Be the person that I'd want to be friends with

7. Embrace my inner 12-year-old

8. Be the person the 20-year-old me would take advice from

9. Be the person that would take advice from the 70-year-old me

10. Be here to give advice when I am 70

11. Wink at those with beautiful souls, not beautiful figures

12. Have great sex

13. Buy name shirts

14. Cash in a regional

15. Not worry about cashing, just throw the ball

16. Accept compliments, don't disagree with them

17.Give Compliments

18. Be here to have game nights with my kids when they are forty

19. Accept that I cannot do it all alone

20.Be strong enough to ask a friend to pour my drink when my hands tremor too badly

21. Repeat #12 as needed

22. Hold doors for how it makes me feel

23. Do stand-up comedy on open mic night

24. Embrace my scars from dermatomyositis

25. Embrace the scars from my journey

26. Get tattoos after I complete #24

27. Complete a half marathon again

28. Wave at those who let me change lanes

29. Pray for those who don't wave at me

30. Get strong enough to work again

31. Talk for hours about nothing

32. Make strangers laugh

33. Laugh at myself, it helps with #32

34. Get back to my fighting weight

35. Be comfortable in my skin if I don't

36. Eat chili in the summer because it is good

37. Eat Ice Cream in the winter because it is good

38. Sing

39. Fall in love with myself

40. Read the Bible from cover to cover

41. Do the things that I love even if I do them poorly.

I had weathered acute Covid. I had gone stir crazy. It was time to start rebuilding. This was no small undertaking. I still got winded by walking to the kitchen, but the clock was ticking. My disability from work was running out and I was nowhere near strong enough to return to work. Where in the world would I start? I'd start from the ground up, literally.

I had ventured to the store a few times and my arms and shoulders were so weak from the dermatomyositis that it was hard to push the shopping cart. I would start with upper body. I started with what was called girl pushups in middle school. I was still reeling with the skin manifestations of dermatomyositis, so I knew that I needed cushion for my knees: I placed a pillow under my knees and attempted the "easy" version of pushups. I got to 4 and collapsed onto my face. I fell asleep on the floor right where I collapsed. I woke up, I don't know how much later. It was my starting point. It was dismal, but it was my baseline.

Chris once again came home from work thinking his best friend had succumbed to Covid, but instead, found me passed out on the floor after one of my 5-10-minute workout sessions. He had a dumbbell set in the garage and helped me move it into my room. I'd work out for 15 minutes and then nap for hours. It was brutal and went on for weeks on end.

February found me entering the public again, not for work, but for rehab. I got my first gym membership in years. I was terrified, but I knew it was necessary. I was still nowhere near strong enough to work in my old position in Dallas. To make matters worse, my position had been vacant too long and I had to step aside, nearly assuring me of a more stressful position whenever I was able to return to work. I had two months, and I was flailing. I had two months, and I knew that I couldn't go back to Texas, back to my ex.

You see, you learn a lot of things when the noises of the day-to-day quiets down. You learn what peace sounds like. You learn that peace isn't just the absence of war. Pease isn't just the absence of damage. Peace is a quiet that is so welcome at first. Peace then becomes deafening as the silence screams the lessons that you couldn't hear over the shelling of everyday life. Peace allows focus and clarity and perhaps most importantly peace allows growth.

~ *Some Things Can't Be Suppressed* ~

I was now clear of the COVID virus, battered and fatigued, but clear of the virus itself. This meant that I could now go back on my immunosuppressive meds to get my dermatomyositis under control. These meds make me so tired, but they are a necessary evil as the disease cannot go unchecked. If not treated, cancer is nearly guaranteed. Even if treated, my cancer risk is 30-40 percent within the next two years. I had no choice but to let it beat me back down further in fatigue. Over the next days, my runs shortened to half mile distances. I was back to yelling in frustration in the darkness of early mornings as I couldn't be in the sunlight for more than 10 minutes without blistering. Depression was setting up shop in my mind again. I was thinking of my demise again. This turned my attention back to the need to finish my book so that just maybe, I could leave some money for my children should I succumb to one of my diseases or to COVID when I got it a third time. This presented a problem, well an opportunity, no it was a problem. I couldn't write about her without her approval. I just stared at her profile picture on Facebook for days.

~ *Good Morning Stranger!* ~

I was getting into my second month of living with Chris and his family. I was grateful. I was also feeling nostalgic being back in Edmond. I was still reeling from COVID but had really been thinking of trying to finish my book. I would need to write about one of the best and worst periods of my life. This involved messaging my first love, my number 1. I had not laid eyes on her or heard her voice in nearly 20 years. I sat in my recliner for what felt like an eternity, trying to gather the strength to message her. All the while remembering how short that I had to been when she messaged me about mom's bible. She was still probably hurt by that or at least a little mad. She probably wouldn't respond. I wanted to write about "us." She shaped me in so many ways, I owed it to her to get it right. I needed her permission. I needed her help. I needed the courage to message my first love after all these years. I simply typed, "Good morning, ma'am" into messenger. I hit send and fully expected no response.

I got one within minutes. "Good morning stranger!" Stranger, that is what she referred to me as before, when she messaged me about mom's bible. She wasn't mad! The relief that I felt was incredible. I was so nervous and knew that I was out of my depth. I was terrified, but I laid it all out there. I told her that I had a question for her. I explained that I had been ill since 2007 and that a year ago my doctor told me that I was on pace to die within 3 years or so. I went on to explain that I was attempting to finish my book, and I could not do so without writing about my first love. That I wanted to do "us" justice. To tell the world about my first love. I needed permission and offered to let her pick the name that I used for her to respect and protect her privacy. She was taken aback. She first asked what was going on with me medically and if I was willing to share that with her. She followed with, "you absolutely can include me and my name. I trust you. I always did." I teared up immediately, she didn't hate me. I still had her trust and maybe I still had a place in her heart. I was so nervous, my hands tremored so badly that I could barely type, but I filled her in on my health struggles since 2007. Her replies once again surprised me.

She was supportive, nonjudgemental and empathetic. She was so kind to me. My nerves began to settle. My hands shook a little less. I then asked her for a favor. She said, "anything…almost!"…I literally laughed out loud as I texted her to be careful. I asked if she'd be willing to send me some of her memories, good or bad, to help my creative process. She agreed and we began to banter back and forth. It was as if we were still those kids that fell in love all those years ago. We didn't miss a beat! The communication was scary good, it was almost too easy. I could feel her smiling as she read my texts. I could hear her laugh and giggle while she read them too! For the first time in 20 years, my heart leapt and raced for all the right reasons. How in the world could this be?

~ I Need a Favor ~

She showed compassion, that wasn't surprising. She then wanted to know that I had a good support system in place, she wanted to make sure that I was being taken care of, day to day, as I battled all these things. My heart melted and sank all at once. I was reluctant to tell her. I mean how do you say that you were homeless, when diagnosed with Covid, if not for the charity of your best friend? I laid it on her. I was honest. I always was with her, no matter the cost. I owed that to her, my first love. I told her about my entire struggle. I let my guard down. I allowed myself to be seen, not as the strong and vibrant man that she loved all those years ago, but as the weaker man who continues to fight just to be here another day. Her reply was better than anything that I could have hoped for.

~ *Memories of US* ~

That night she kept her word to me. She sent me an e-mail of her memories of "us" to help me write my book. Her unedited email follows:

So many memories flooding back! Most of them are so, so good. Then a few painful

ones mixed in. Hope these make you smile, giggle, cry and feel absolutely LOVED as

They have made me feel reminiscing. Feel free to share what you want. Like I said- I

trust you.

I remember small things that are so random like eating spaghetti noodles for dinner with

no sauce since we both didn't like it.

I remember big obstacles like you getting Chicken pox coming back from one of our

trips and everyone trying to keep me from you but also everyone telling me to get

exposed to you since I hadn't had it and it's better when I am young. You were so sick. I just wanted to be there with you and try to take care of you. We exposed me to the virus

then- and I didn't get it and I still to this day have never had chicken pox.

I remember our first weekend…ya know. It was amazing. And I remember you had to

keep running to that little gas station by the apartment to get more condoms…while I sat

in a cold tub hoping to get the swelling down. We didn't even leave the apartment other

than for that- and maybe 1 meal…to go. Lol

I remember planning a Christmas wedding- then getting into a big fight before you

dropped me off at the mall for work and me giving you my ring back. Felt like my world

ended. I was devastated. But we worked things out.

We drove for what felt like forever in your mom's van with your mom to VEGAS baby! We were so young! I carried a little cup around Caesar's Palace of coins, we took some pictures on the rooftop, then I proudly watched you compete.

Oh, my goodness! Remember when we lived in the double wide- left for a tournament,

lost our clothes! Went to Walmart in the middle of the night for shirts/ iron on letters and had to make your shirt. Man…talk about thinking outside the box! Together I felt like we

were unstoppable.

You spoiled me rotten any chance you got. You bought me several gifts one year for

Christmas early in our relationship. Took me on a date then gave them to me to

open afterwards. I was staying at my cousin's house in Lexington. I still have the Victoria

Secret cosmetic bag and use it often.

I remember going to your mom's barber shop and watching her cut your hair, then you

cutting your own hair after her passing.

I loved the days you let me ride with you on your route. Seeing everything in the middle

of nowhere. Talking for hours.

I remember the day you lost your mom. It still kills me that I was the reason you all were

fighting. I remember our last time seeing her we were at their house, and I was sitting in

the jeep- and she was screaming and trying to climb into the back of it. She was so mad at me for taking you away from her. I am so sorry about that. I am so sorry I didn't do

everything in my power to assure her that I would never do that. I also remember sitting

on our couch and your phone ringing and you saying you weren't' going to answer

because it was her. She called again, and you didn't answer. Then someone else

called- you answered, and they said we better get to the hospital in Edmond. That your

mom wasn't doing well. We left and drove as fast as we could. You kept saying she was

just wanting attention and that she is fine, and I agreed with you. I will never forget

getting off the elevator and hearing a woman yelling NO. You looked at me into my eyes

and said someone just died. Then we walked around the corner, and it was your family.

We didn't believe it. It wasn't possible. I remember having to chase you down the hall-

You were so upset. Punching things. Crying. Devastating. Blood was all over my jacket

from me holding you and your nose bleeding. I still have that jacket too.

You would move mountains to see me. When I lived in Shawnee you would drive early,

early in the morning to see. You would drive late at night after work to come see me. It was close to an hour's drive from you, but you still made it- often.

After I had moved out and we were apart for a bit, I remember you picking me up when I

worked at the check cashing place. We didn't have anywhere we were going but just for

a drive and you told me you were filing for a divorce- and you had met someone. I didn't

even know what to say or how to respond but I understood. I asked to keep my name

Pride. You fought that at first but that was who I was. Misty Pride. Then I remember the

day you showed up to bring me the divorce papers for me to sign. We stepped outside-

The sun was shining, and I signed them. Then you left. Shortly after that I moved to

Tulsa alone knowing no one and cried every night for weeks.

You were such a great man, great friend, great husband. I am sure you have become a

great father. You swept me off my feet and then did everything you could to keep me

floating on LOVE. I felt that when I was with you. Never did I doubt your love for me. I

hope you felt my love for you. You will ALWAYS have a place in my heart that is carved

out for you- my first love.

~ Tears ~

I could barely read her e-mail through my tears. I could feel how much she loved me. I was amazed at how much of "us" she had kept tucked away in her heart all these years. Perhaps she had thought of me as much as I had thought of her over the past 20 years. I was distraught over lost time. I was humbled by her love. I stared at her profile picture. It wasn't just her. She had built a life for herself. In fact, she has done so multiple times over the years. I knew this because I checked her profile periodically over the years. She looked happy and that is exactly the existence that I wanted for her. That's what she deserved. She deserved more than the life that I could provide. She deserved someone strong, like the guy that shared her Facebook profile picture, her husband. Besides, I gave up that title in 1999.

Do you remember that scene in the Matrix when the oracle tells Neo not to worry about the vase? He said, what vase? As he turns and knocks it over and it shatters. He then asks, how did you? Then she says, "I told you not to worry about it." Then proceeds to tell him, what is really gonna cook your noodle later is if you would have still broken it if I hadn't said anything. My mother's passing is the vase in my first marriage. We would never know the outcome if the vase hadn't shattered. It was each of our first loves. First loves are magnificent and passionate, not all are meant to last. I don't blame her, if anything, I blame myself. As time passes you can look back and wonder, but you can never wander the same roads again for the first time. She taught me how to love and for that I am grateful. She taught me pain and for that I am grateful too. It took years to realize why Dec 2, 1998, was so cataclysmic for me. I lost my mother and my first love, in the same moment.

~ It's Okay ~

The next day I had to let her know. I had to let her know that I forgave her. After reading her e-mail, I knew that she blamed herself for how painful the events of my mother's passing were for me. I messaged her to let her know that I forgave her and that it was all on me. That I didn't want her carrying that weight around any longer. She told me that I never verbally blamed her, but she felt a distance between us after my mother passed.

The seriousness soon gave way to reminiscing of the good ole days again. We joked back and forth for days. Crossing no lines, we bonded again, quickly. She had me laughing so much, more than I had in 20 years. She was laughing too; I just knew it. More and more memories came to mind, even one that I once again needed to get permission to include. This would push a boundary, or so I thought.

I asked her if I could respectfully write about "just don't move." It would be giving me permission to write about the time that we lost our virginity to each other. Her reply was immediate, "yes!" This gave way to recalling just how amazing our chemistry had been. How we might argue for an hour, but then we'd spend a weekend making love. I put it out there that I had never had another lover that compared to her and held my breath while I watched her text bubbles. She confirmed that she felt the same way. We had just officially, undeniably, flirted.

~ I'm Not Here to Fuck Your Shit Up ~

She called me on it by texting, "flirtation meter spiking!" I told her that I would stop if she wanted me to, as I just swung for the fence in all that I do now. Her reply shook me, she replied, "I am extremely torn." My heart sank and then I saw more text bubbles and I waited for what seemed like an eternity to see her next message. It populated, "keep swinging for the fence!" I had a numbered reply which was as follows:

1. I'm not here to fuck your shit up

2. You are the one that got away

3. You are the one that got away

She then admitted that her brain was in overdrive since my first message to her. I explained that I knew that there was no way that our marriage would have ended if mom hadn't died the way that she did. She agreed 100%. I asked how her brain was doing; it wasn't any better. I asked her if she wanted to take some time to think things over. She simply replied with a thinking emoji. What was I thinking? This was no time to sit back, hell I could be dead next week. I immediately followed with, "you look good by the way, not helping, I know, but you really do." Her reply floored me.

She said that it also wasn't helping that she was going to be in OKC that week. She also said that it didn't help that her marriage had not been going well for a long time. All of this and simultaneously, she was telling me that she was going to be close to me. I couldn't help myself; I had to joke and swing for the fence again. I told her that if she'd buy me dinner that I'd put out, sorry not sorry. Then I waited.

"Um no dinner, no putting out. Definitely, not helping." Over the next few days, we continued to joke back and forth, but I did something that also came naturally to me as well. I told her exactly what I saw. She worked so hard to get to where she was today. She was amazing, talented, confident and beautiful. I told her all these things. She took the compliments and thanked me. Then fate intervened, this time in my favor. She messaged me furious. I couldn't believe it.

~ *Gorgeous No Matter What* ~

It was true. I always thought that she was beautiful, no matter what. Blonde, brunette or red she was always "gorgeous" to me. In fact, I never called her by her name, I called her gorgeous because that is exactly what she was, no matter what. She messaged me furious…with a selfie.

You see, I had never seen her with her hair this short. She had an undercut, where the sides of her head were clipper cut with relatively short hair on top. Still smoking hot, gorgeous no matter what. Her hubby as it turns out liked her hair short and called her "shaggy" that morning. Obviously not the brightest crayon in the 64-pack box. Who the fuck was he looking at? She was perfect. She apologized for venting; I was dumbfounded by his blindness.

She told me she knew that I could tell that she was mad by how red her neck was at that moment. There was another emotion that turned her neck red, and I told her about it in my reply, "or really turned on." She was taken aback by how well I still knew her. I told her that those things about her were engraved in my memory. We began to reminisce about our first time again and how nobody else ever came close to matching what we had together. She ended our conversation by telling me that she was slipping into her hot tub, an overt supplying of an image to me and I called her on it. She said, "enjoy the image I am in it often." She was now pushing the envelope a bit and I liked it. She was not being appreciated and that provided more rationalization to me that our flirting was justified, not that I needed any help in the rationalization department. I still felt like I was at death's door, and she was breathing life into me, one memory and one text at a time.

~ *Is That a Proposal?* ~

We started chatting early the following day. She filled me in on her day, she was so damn impressive. She was a powerful woman. Confident, unapologetic, just sexy as hell. I told her that she was all those things and how proud I was of the amazing woman that she was just in case she hadn't heard that lately, she said that she sure hadn't heard that at all. I just shook my head, he had no concept of how amazing she really was, how lucky that he should consider himself. Just a fucking fool that didn't even come close to deserving a woman like her. She then asked if I wanted to chat in person the next day.

She reminded me of our reminiscing session at Denny's all those years ago. How we didn't cross any lines, and we could do something like that again. I had to break the bad news to her. There was something that she wasn't thinking about.

I reminded her that restaurants and bars were out of the question as I was severely immunocompromised. She felt terrible. She felt selfish for not thinking of how sick she could make me. Afterall, she traveled constantly, exposing herself to everything. She said she wanted to see a kind face and get a bearhug from me and just wasn't thinking. I told her that we could talk on the phone. I wanted to hear her voice so badly. She said she could let me meet her at her hotel, but that was "dangerous" for both of us. I told her to call me and if it went well and if she felt comfortable that she could invite me over and I'd bring dinner.

She gave me her number and told me to call her. I was so nervous that I could barely dial her number. I don't even really remember what we talked about. I just remember laughing for 45 minutes and more importantly, hearing that giggle that I had missed so much over the last 20 years. By the end of the night, she told me that I could meet her at her hotel as she had some things that she was going through that she wanted to talk to me about. For the first time in 20 years, I was going to see Misty.

~ Forecast? 100% Misty ~

I awoke the next morning feeling more filled with life than I had since 2007, hell since 1999. I was meeting her at her hotel. She would not be in my car. I washed and detailed it out, as if she would be. I asked her, red or white? She loved Moscato, just like me. The day flew by as we bantered back and forth. I was so excited, so was she. I was beside myself. I had no intention of making a move on her, truthfully no intention. I just wanted to see her, to hear her voice, her giggle. Before I knew it, it was time to drive to her. I made my way to her hotel. Panic fully set in as I pulled into the parking lot. My hands shook terribly as I made my way down the hall to her room. I had a bottle of wine in each trembling hand, leaving me no free hand to knock on the door. I tried to tap on the door with the bottom of a wine bottle but tremored so badly that it banged loudly against the door. The door opened and there stood my first love.

I was floored by how good she looked, just as gorgeous as she had always been, but this time, even better. In traditional Misty fashion, she opened the conversation by giving me shit. She said, "that's how you knock on the door?" I tried to fill the air with conversation explaining that I had no free hand as I tried to hurry to get the wine glasses and wine bottles out of my hands before she saw how bad I was shaking. I didn't want her to see how badly I was damaged physically. I set everything down and turned around and was met with the hug that I had been waiting 20 years to receive.

I held her and frankly never wanted to let her go. I did though, I looked at her and told her how great she looked and waited for her to blush, she did. I scanned the room for a table, there wasn't one. I scanned for chairs, there was only one. That left just the bed. She knew it though, and she didn't look like she minded one bit, I pointed out the obvious and we each sat at the end of the bed, I couldn't believe what happened next.

We sat at the end of the bed, and we made eye contact. She moved her leg as if to throw it over the top of mine just like the old days. I was completely taken aback, but I didn't dare call her on it. It might have simply been a reflex, just an involuntary example of muscle memory from all those years ago. But if it wasn't, my God what if it wasn't?

I tried to break the tension, as she saw me look at her when she tried to lay her leg over the top of mine. I asked if she wanted to go ahead and have some wine. She readily agreed. She had already seen my tremors and I had told her previously that I may need help with certain things. I asked if she minded opening the wine, I hated to ask, I hated to look weak. But I made myself vulnerable to her. She leapt at the chance to show her willingness to help me, to be a partner.

~ *The Best Thing That Never Happened* ~

I just gazed at her as she used the corkscrew to open the first bottle of wine. It wouldn't cooperate. She then set it aside, giving up on it and moving to the next. It too would not cooperate. She told me that it wasn't looking like it was going to happen. I was determined to make this happen. I was far too nervous to proceed without having something to calm my nerves. However, all that happened was that we shredded the tops of each of the corks. Completely sober conversation was the only option. I was terrified.

We began talking, small talk of course. We got about 20 minutes into our conversation and then I had to ask her something that I really wasn't comfortable asking her, but I had to ask. She might think I'm being forward, but I am not trying to be. I go ahead and ask her. My back was hurting as it always did, I asked if I could lay down. I know, I know it seems like I was playing a game, but I wasn't. She did not hesitate, she said, "of course." We made our way up to the pillows and our eyes locked when they made contact.

We talked about me. We explored my struggles, my triumphs and tragedies. I told her everything. I hated to tell her about my pain. Every word that I said, I could see my pain expressed in her eyes. She hated to hear everything that I had been through. She wanted desperately to erase it all from my history, but she knew that she couldn't. It meant the world to me that she cared so much. It had been so long since someone cared that much about me, but now it was my turn to listen to what she needed me to hear about what she had been dealing with for so long.

She too laid it all out there. No hesitation at all, but that is how we always were. Honest, brutal and passionate in everything that we did. She explained that she wasn't 'really' married. They had no children together. She explained how he didn't legally divorce his previous wife before he took his sacred vows with MY soulmate. He didn't value her enough, my thoughts, not her words. How in the fuck was she not worth the effort, worth the honesty?

She went on to explain that he did give her a disclaimer that he was an asshole, though deep down she thought he was being facetious. He wasn't. He wasn't abusive but was not a partner in any other sense of the word other than throwing money at some bills. She works hard, too hard in fact. A high stress career and a side hustle that has her pulling 17 to18 hour days regularly. She does all of this and then does the yardwork, dishes, laundry, cooking…all of it, while he hasn't made effort to help her in any way in quite some time. It seemed like a passive aggressive punishment of sorts, like he wanted it over and just wanted her to pull the trigger to end their relationship. He wasn't even man enough to help her do that task either. Then there's something even worse.

He doesn't love her for who she is, for who she wants to be. So, in fact, he doesn't really love her at all. To the point that she has a tattoo on the most beautiful collar bone in the world that states, "Love me for me." How could he not do just that? She is amazing and always has been, but even more so now. She had survived abusive relationships, that just tore my heart into a million pieces. She is worth the effort. She is amazing and as the hours rolled by, I could feel the pain in her voice, in her soul, as she recounted the last 20 years of her life without me. The tragedy and pain that she had been going through mirrored my own struggles. Each of us had been trying to check in on each other over the past 20 years, without speaking. Each of us had been scared to hurt the other's happiness in any way if the other was in a great relationship and had a happy home. Each of us longing for how good it used to feel to be together, not even knowing the other was struggling so badly just to hold it together in the other's absence. We had a deeper conversation over a span of 7 hours than we could have ever wished for had we managed to open those bottles of wine. Turns out, failing to get those bottles open was the best thing that could have happened.

~ *Can I Kiss Her?* ~

We had now laid on our sides, eyes locked, talking for 8 hours. As it was in our past, we were going to be together, it was a foregone conclusion. I rested my hand on her hip. This was the first time that I had the privilege of doing that in 20 years. We continued to talk, each wanting to kiss, each too scared to do so, until I wasn't. I took her face into my hands while she was midsentence. I kissed her. I kissed the love of my life. I kissed her because I had been waiting 20 years for this moment.

I will never forget the feeling of kissing her. It was as if for the first time in 20 years, that my heart, my mind and my soul relaxed. We both exhaled at the same time, like we had crossed a finish line that we never thought that we'd get to cross again. We had each gone through so much and the feeling of being completely vulnerable in the arms of each other, in the arms of someone that we knew would never hurt us is simply something that could never be done justice with words.

Before we knew it, the sun was rising, and she had to get ready to go her way and I had to go mine. I did, however, get to spend the morning getting ready and more importantly, I got to watch her get ready. She was magnificent, truly something to behold. She was everything that I always knew that I wanted, but more than that she was now everything that I never knew I needed in a partner. Just perfection. We talked as adults, lovers, but also as best friends again. She held my heart in her hands, just as she always had and I trusted her with it completely, as I always had.

Our morning passed too quickly as well. She was worried about me, that was easy to see. I loved that she still cared so deeply, but I hated to see that look of worry in her eyes. I begged her to let me go get her coffee and she rebuffed me. She barely let me carry her bag to her car, but I just had to do something for her. She looked me in the eyes and kissed me. She asked if it would be okay that it took a while for us to be together. She went on to say that she had things to take care of, that she was going through the separation process and that it would take time, but we would get there. She gave me a look that told me that it was real, that this wasn't just one night for her either.

~ I've Got You ~

My kiddos came to visit me in early February. It was the first time that they spent any real amount of time with me in a while. I remember lying in the recliner, still bleeding through my clothes in spots and my daughter standing over me. She said, "dad, when you beat it this time. When you get strong enough to go back to work and I KNOW you will. You get your first tattoo. I want you to get UNKILLABLE somewhere on your body, because that is what you are, remember?" I grinned and agreed.

I was still shaky and weak, but we played video games, and I cooked with Serenity like we used to do. I told them about my New Year's Resolutions and being better about asking for help when I needed it. Here's the thing about kids, they listen.

We were laughing, joking and I was singing around the kitchen island. It was the best time that I had in years. We were making our favorite gluten free dinner, my famous homemade pizza from scratch. It takes a lot of energy, but it was worth it to have some sense of normalcy for myself and more importantly for my children. The fatigue fully set in once we got to the topping phase of our wheatless masterpiece. My hands were too weak to open the bag of cheese. I turned my back toward the kiddos to hide the frustration and kept trying. I fumbled and fumbled, getting more upset that I still couldn't do such a simple task. Upset that I still wasn't making the strides that I desperately needed to make to regain my old version of normalcy, then I looked up. My son had made his way across the kitchen. He gently put his hands around mine and said, "I've got you dad." My autistic son, had the empathy and wherewithal to see his father struggling and with so much compassion he helped me through an oddly rough moment that few others would understand. I finished topping the pizza and went to the bathroom and ugly cried with pride. That moment will be forever etched in my memory as one of my favorite moments with my son.

~ *Worth the Drive* ~

Over a hundred miles separated Misty and me. We messaged and talked every single chance we got. We laughed like teenagers, we flirted like newlyweds and started planning like partners. Our messages and conversations became cravings that couldn't be satisfied fully without being able to physically touch each other. We both had a desperate need to see each other in person again. She had a plan, a plan that mother nature would test.

The time when our schedules allowed, I also needed to drive to Texas to pick up my kids for them to stay with me for a week. It would take me an hour and a half to get to her and there was weather moving in. Between the weather and the miles that I needed to drive, we'd only get to see each other for about an hour. She worried about me being tired. I assured her that just getting to see her would provide all the energy that I needed.

I arrived at the meet point before she did, I was not going to miss a moment with her. I was a nervous wreck, but I was there. She arrived and I was breathless. I met her at her car door and hugged her, the kind of hug that you never want to end.

Like it always does when we are together, the time just flew by. It was time to part, but she was already planning our next meeting. We would meet once a week, just to get our fix, not of sex, but to simply be able to hold each other, to gaze into to each other's eyes and feel wholly complete if only for an hour at a time. We had something even better on the horizon to look forward to in the coming months.

We continued our messages and calls of encouragement and love throughout the days and nights when we couldn't get to each other. She began to encourage me to bowl again, to practice when we met. She watched me, like she used to do 20 years ago. The feeling of turning around after throwing a shot and seeing her was just like the rest of our relationship, simply phenomenal. Soon we would get to take a trip together.

~ Atlanta ~

We couldn't get the same flight out as I couldn't get to her until the following day, but she relished the opportunity to pick me up at the airport. It would be the first time for me on a plane since COVID hit, since beating my second bout of it. Being immunocompromised, flying commercially was the last place in the world that I should be, but it was where I absolutely had to be. There was no place in the world that I would rather be. I was bound and determined to get to my soulmate.

The feeling of landing at my destination was nothing other than that pure excitement and anticipation. I asked her what kind of car she was in, and she told me it was a white kia. For the record, you really have no idea how many white Kias there are rolling around Atlanta until you are waiting for your soulmate to roll up in one. I felt like a dog watching his owner eat, hopeful at every glimpse of what I thought was going to be my "piece." I was pathetic and kept talking to her on the phone, "I see you!" nope, I see you now, nope. We laughed at my awkwardness much like we did when we were young.

She did finally roll up and I practically ran to her car. I hopped in and she simply said, "hey baby!" and kissed me. It was amazing just to have her with me again, but to see the excitement in her eyes when she saw me meant the world to me.

~ *A Different Dynamic* ~

I had NEVER ridden with her as a passenger, like EVER. She was weaving in and out of traffic like a stock car driver. It started out frightening, but then she started multitasking. She was taking business calls, cussing and owning the highways of Atlanta all at the same time. I just sat back and watched her in amazement in all her lead footed, foul-mouthed glory.

We were driving on fumes and pushed toward a gas station in downtown Atlanta. Of course, their pumps were going on and offline and Misty was starting to worry that we'd run out of gas in downtown Atlanta. She was a bit distracted when her iPhone lit up with a Facetime request. She looked at me and said, "be quiet, it's my daughter." My volume turned out not to be our biggest concern.

Her daughter knew my name, as Misty had talked about me over the years. She had not let her daughter know that she was seeing anyone so quickly as she had gone from one relationship to another, much like I had over the years. Each of us trying over and over to find "us" in another relationship. Quiet is easy, well for me it can be a challenge sometimes. However, I was silent, motionless as I pretended to not exist as I heard her daughter's voice for the first time. Misty kept looking at the gas pump and when she turned her head, she also turned her phone's camera toward me. Panic set in! Hi! I'm new step-daddy!

That's what I would have to say, my running joke with Misty was that I would refer to her as new step-mommy to my kids once we broke the news. When in actuality no one else, besides my best friend, knew we were together. Instead, I lunged at the phone to redirect it. She did this to me two more times. Hilarious now, but God almighty I think I had 3 strokes in 48 seconds.

We made it to the hotel parking garage, and I grabbed my bag and hers. She wasn't pleased that I was trying to do so much, but I wouldn't give her a say in the matter. One of my favorite moments was when we were walking down the street holding hands. We looked at each other, locked eyes and grinned. We were exactly where we were supposed to be, not Atlanta, but simply with each other.

We got to the room and settled in quickly. There was no tension, none. We had waited for this for weeks. I lay on the bed, and she turned on the TV. I watched her click through the guide. We hadn't watched TV together for 20 years.

I saw the Big Bang Theory and wanted her to pick it but said nothing. The Misty I remembered would have loved it. I just waited to see what she would pick. She did pick it. We cuddled up and giggled and laughed together, just like the old days, but better. Again, we had conversations and shared the kind of kisses that they only write about in books.

We had a view of the Atlanta skyline; we had thunder and flashes of lighting. I wrapped my arms around her while she stood at the window. We were both in awe of how perfect our night together was becoming as each second passed by us. We made love. This time better than ever. We shared passion, orgasms and giggles over and over in no particular order. We laughed until we cried, we gave ourselves to each other until we were spent. It was everything we wanted. It was everything that we needed.

Once again time passed too fast. I haven't been able to fall asleep quickly since 2007. She wanted me to try to sleep as she knew that I don't sleep much. I laid back and wrapped my arm around her. She laid her head on my chest. I relaxed completely and drifted off in seconds. I felt safe with her, no matter where we were, if I was with her. I was home!

~ Coffee? I've Got You ~

The next morning, we began to get ready, this time we got to catch the same flight. We got the opportunity to do all the little things together. This was a little different, this time she asked me if I would mind going to Starbucks and getting her a Chai Tea and some egg bites. I leapt at the chance. It allowed her to finish getting ready and it allowed me to do something for her. I got back and gave her breakfast to her. She looked at me and said thank you, I said, it is literally nothing. She disagreed. She hadn't had someone care enough to get her coffee in years. I hated that, as she is more spectacular than she will ever realize.

We arrived at the airport and had to ride the railway tram. She looked at me worried when we started moving. She was worried about my balance as I am still wobbly from all my nerve damage and vertigo. I refused to sit. I refused to look that frail. We started to move, and I swayed. She didn't tell me to sit. Instead, she wrapped her arms around me, to give me support and gave me a look that said, "I've got you." I loved her even more for that than I already did, and I didn't think that was even possible.

We made our way through the airport. You know that you are with the right person when you are the only ones laughing their way through the TSA Checkpoint. We walked through the airport holding hands completely lost in each other's eyes. Every little experience was magical if we were together.

The flight went smoothly and quickly. We had time to eat lunch on her layover before we had to part ways. We chose Mexican food. We sat there and did all the things that we do every time we were together. We laughed, we kissed and had serious conversations about our plans. She had a lot of things to take care of, to be free of the obstacles in her way. I had obstacles of my own. I had moved states and would need to get licensed so I could stay close to her. I would inform my best friend as to how all of life's wrong turns were now starting to make sense. As with so many perfectly laid plans, they would change.

~ *Best Laid Plans* ~

My best friend was overjoyed that I had once again found happiness in my personal life. My spirits had been lifted, but now he knew why. It lifted his spirits as well, that is a true friend. Then, I got the news. It was Misty. She was going to end her separation and not move forward with divorce proceedings. He had taken her to dinner and begged her back. He agreed to work on himself and be a better man for her. She was caught between feeling like a three-time failure in marriage and failing her first love. I hoped and prayed that he would keep his word, even though I was devastated, I was not angry. I could never be angry with her. I responded that I understood and that he was a better bet in terms of longevity and while anyone could get hit by a bus tomorrow, my lifespan was all but guaranteed to be much shorter with all my health issues. I stepped aside without argument, without making a case for myself. I would have loved to have her as a partner, but here is the thing about chronic illness and pain. It doesn't just affect you; it affects those around you, those that love you. While heartbroken, I was grateful for the time that we spent together, for the hope that got me through some of my darkest hours, but also that she wouldn't have front row seats to watch me deteriorate faster than a man of my age should. I was grateful that she wouldn't have to watch helplessly as that would surely occur. Hell, I wasn't even certain that I could get healthy enough to work full time again. She deserved someone who could contribute more to her life than I thought that I could. She didn't need any more weight to carry on my behalf. Those are the thought processes of the chronically ill that creep into your love life. I let her go without any contestation. I let her go because I loved her.

I broke the news to Chris and the fear and disappointment on his face, in his eyes were palpable. He asked if I was okay, mentally. I shrugged my shoulders and went to bed. The next morning, we crossed paths in the kitchen. He said, "where are you off to this morning brother?" I said, "got to get my physical rehab in, my kiddos need me strong." He shook his head, and asked, "how do you achieve that level of self-love? You just lost the love of your life for the second time." I said, "I keep waking up, so as long as I do that, I am going to keep fighting to stay here."

She would reach out a couple years later. He didn't change, folks rarely do. She said that she walked around with regret over her decision. I regretted it too. Sometimes, no matter how badly we want something, no matter how right it feels, the universe has other plans. Just like that scene from the Matrix with the vase, my mother's passing set in motion a chain of events where our timelines would never match up. Both of us have now divorced 3 times, each of us wondering what each of our worlds would be like had the vase not broken that fateful day in December all those years ago. Chris' question about self-love was not just a quip, it was intensely personal.

~ *Porridge* ~

Chris had been fighting his own war for quite some time. He and his wife had been together for 25 years. They married young and he will be first to admit that he had more than a few indiscretions and made more than his share of mistakes early in their marriage. They had moved past it. She had forgiven him, or so he thought.

Early in my battle with COVID. I heard it, I heard all of it. She still lived there; they pretended that they were okay at first. I went along with it at first. I was probably too busy trying to die the first couple of weeks to hear it. But as I recovered, I could hear the fighting between midnight and 5 am nearly every night. It was heart-breaking. I couldn't make out much, but she hurled curse words at him like the bullies hurled dodge balls at the unpopular kids in 6th grade PE. It was relentless, there was no intention to solve anything, no lumber used to build bridges, its only intention was to cause pain.

She was baiting him. She was punishing him. He had hurt her, now after years of doing the right things, now was the time that she had chosen to start punishing him. He loved her and he was in a panic. It was hard to watch. One morning she walked through the kitchen, he told her good morning, she replied with "go fuck yourself!" It was over, but he couldn't accept it, not yet.

Night after night, when he would get home from work, she would attack him, attack him when he was at his most exhausted. Night after night, I would counsel him to accept that his run was over. He would beg her to love him, to make it work, he would do anything.   She wanted nothing to do with him. Again, at night, I would hear it from my recliner that had been my home for weeks. I called it porridge.

If you remember Oliver Twist, he asked the mean woman for more porridge, despite it being awful. That's what I told him he was doing, that he was embarrassing himself by asking for something that was awful. He was always strong, always callous, but now I told him that he was weak, that he was a disappointment to me. That got his attention. Then later that night, I heard someone ring the doorbell at 1 am. I saw someone looking through the windows.

~ *The Right of Silence* ~

Someone was trying to get into the house. How was I the only one hearing it. I limped to Chris' room and told him the situation and asked if he had a gun. He got his gun and we both went to the door. He then realized who was outside and slid the gun onto the kitchen table. This just got interesting, but it was about to get terrifying.

He opened the door to reveal 2 policemen that asked him his name. He replied honestly, they told him that he had the right to remain silent and that they had a warrant for him on the charge of domestic violence. This had to be a mistake, right?

It was indeed a mistake, but then again, it wasn't. He and his wife had argued one night in September, she hit him, she charged at him, he moved out of the way, and she fell and hit her head. She called the police and lied and said that he had hit her and threw her down. The warrant was an error. He had been cleared, but that didn't matter. I watched in bewilderment as he was taken away in cuffs.

He was MY support system; I was like Richard Gere in an Officer and a Gentleman. I had nowhere else to go. I looked at his wife and had a very real conversation. I asked her if she knew what would happen if he lost his job. I told her that she, her daughter and I would all be homeless. I told her that her bullshit was now impacting my life too. I asked, "are you ready to live on the fucking street, because I'm not!"

I stood there, covered in blood blisters, bleeding through my shirt and pants, wondering what the fuck I was going to do. When morning came, I did the only rational thing that I could think of, and I called his father. He had been the point man in September when this all started. Chris wouldn't be released until midnight. He spent 23 hours in the county jail. I didn't want her to pick him up. As I knew how she would treat him. He was fragile before being handcuffed in front of his best friend; I couldn't imagine what his state would be like when he got to walk out of that place. So, with COVID, I drove to the county jail and waited. I had a plan.

I knew that he would be embarrassed. I needed a segue. I needed a way to break the ice. I got an idea to do just that. When he finally walked out to the car and opened the door, he was greeted with the musical styles of the Ghetto Boys, damn it feels to be a gangster. He grinned and leaned against me and said, "I love you brother." I had my best friend doing exactly what I wanted, he was smiling despite his circumstance.

~ Gains and Groceries ~

After weeks of trying to workout at home, in my cave, it was time to venture out. I knew that I was stronger than I had been, but nowhere near strong enough to go back to work yet. I pulled into a parking lot and my hands shook as I placed a mask over my face. To get the strength that I needed, going back into the public space was unavoidable. I limped into Gold's gym and started the next phase of my journey to get my life back.

I took the tour and looked at all the contact surfaces with a sense of foreboding and fear. The feeling of putting my health in danger, to start rebuilding my life was daunting. With a slide of a credit card, it was done.

It was daunting but gave me a sense of purpose. I had a starting point other than running. I needed to combat muscle weakness and the only way to do that was to do resistance training. Something that I despised, but my disgust with weakness outweighed how much I despised the iron.

Day in and day out, I stumbled, literally stumbled through the gym. I was so exhausted that it wasn't an uncommon occurrence for someone to wake me up on a machine. Yes, I would literally pass out in between sets. I slowly gained strength, but only because I had nothing else to concentrate on besides getting better. I would train then go home and sleep. Then something happened, or should I say something didn't happen.

I checked my account and my short-term disability from my employer did not hit our account. I scrambled and made phone calls. My doc had faxed updates, but they claimed not to have received them. It took days to get a straight answer. My boss caught wind of it and called me. It would be 2 weeks before it would start back up again, what he said next blew me away.

He said, make me a list. I asked what? He said, "make me a list, take your time and make me a list of the food that you and your family need for the next 30 days. Do not leave anything out." He said that he was blessed financially and would not take no for an answer. I made the list, and he kept my family fed as I continued to fight to get better. It was once again emasculating, but I was grateful for his kindness. If you are reading this, thank you Aman.

~ *Dad Needs Me* ~

Those are the words that my son said in late February. He said, "dad needs me, and he shouldn't be alone." I had been homeschooling my son, even before COVID, and I had been helping him when he'd come visit or from afar, but not nearly enough. So, my ex agreed with his wishes as I would also be in a better position to help him stay caught up and to take the responsibility off of her plate. I had room for him, and he became my roommate in the mother-in-law wing of Chris' home. I had my son back and for that I was grateful. We just did life together, day in and day out. He'd do his schoolwork as best he could while I trained and then I'd help him finish up. When that was done, we'd watch movies or play a game. One night I was watching a movie and he walked into the room and said something that shook me.

He said, "you know what dad? It is just calmer here. No drama, no fighting, it is just calmer, and I like it." I grinned and hugged him and at the same time, it hurt my soul. I stayed with Allie for the kids. I stayed for 7 years after the affair. I was the one who did the homework. I was the one who went on field trips. I was the one who packed lunches. I was the one who drove them to school. Dads don't get custody, and I wasn't about to only see them a few days a month. So, I stayed, but we argued. He felt a difference in the existence of me without my ex. I couldn't change the past, but damn it made me wonder if I had made the right choice. I would get my answer during my daughter's next visit.

~ The Looks and the Nods ~

Serenity would come and visit every couple of weeks. Our bonding time consisted of zombies and cooking. An odd combo? Yes, but those were our things. I had worked on perfecting my gluten free pizza for a decade and it was once again their request one Saturday night. It was an exhausting process even on my best of days, but I was not about to say no to my kiddos getting some sense of normalcy. I was knee deep in the Pillsbury Doughboy when their mom called. I was cordial, I had achieved some level of self-control after her abandoning me in my moment of need. She was on the speakerphone and said, "you know, you can still come home, and we can be a family again." I immediately looked across the kitchen island at my kiddos. In unison, without looking at each other, they looked at me with the most serious expressions I had ever seen them muster and both nodded no. She said, "well you're going to have to come back to Texas to work and we can't afford for you to have two places. You will have to move in with me. You are not licensed to practice in Oklahoma." She was right. I made pizza and played games and watched zombies...then I went to Chris.

I had two months of disability left. It was barely enough to cover alimony and child support. I paid no rent. I paid no utilities. I had the audacity to tell him I needed money to get licensed in Oklahoma. He didn't hesitate. He said, "brother, you'll die if you go back to a toxic environment. You are finally starting to get better." Then the next morning he put hundreds of dollars in my hand and said, "get it done brother." I explained that I had to pass my Oklahoma Law exam to get licensed here. He said, "you're like Harry Stamper, you don't know how to fail. You've never failed a test in your life." I said, "well I've never taken a board exam with COVID brain either." He said, "there is no way on Earth that you will fail when your kids need you to pass."

~ If You Had One Shot ~

If you had one shot. One opportunity to seize everything you wanted....I was sick, but desperately needed to get licensed in Oklahoma. That meant studying for my law exam, homeschooling my son and training all at the same time. It would push me harder than I needed to be pushed at this point, but there was no other choice. It was a proving ground as to whether I could add more and more to my plate and tolerate it. I paid my fees and waited for the authorization to test.

For the first time since moving in with Chris, I started setting an alarm clock. I started at 5:30 am with the gym. Then home to study. I'd see Chris as he went to work and when he'd get home at night. He'd still find me studying. Day after day, it was the same. He asked if I had it down after a week. I told him that my COVID fog was so bad that I wasn't retaining anything. He said, "it is in there somewhere." I got the authorization to test in record time. I wasn't getting any better and scheduled it as fast as I could. Was it wise? No. Did I rationalize it? Yes.

The rationalization was this, I felt shackled to Texas, to my ex. I did not want to go back. She made her choice. She had told me to leave for years, I just didn't take her up on it. I stayed for the kids. This time, I am staying away for the sake of the kids. The cold hard truth was that the kids were better off with us being apart. I wanted the shackles off as soon as possible. I desperately needed to grasp some shred of dignity and freedom. I studied harder. I paced through the house all day for days on end, desperately trying to get the info to stick in my head, so that I would not have to go back to Texas with my tail between my legs. Before I knew it, test day was upon me.

The first date available was at a location that was about a 45-minute drive for me. My head was still spinning between vertigo and brain fog, the drive was over in an instant. I walked into the center, presented my ID, put my belongings in a locker and they scanned my fingerprints. It was go-time, and I was exhausted before I answered the first question.

Question after question, I would talk myself into and out of answers. The brain fog was in full affect, adrenaline was pumping like crazy, and I was not confident when I walked out the door. I drove back home and plopped into the recliner that I had fought so hard to get out of months earlier. Within moments, there was a knock on the door. I said, "come in" and Chris and his wife opened the door. Chris said, "How do you feel about it." I said, "I think I failed, for the first time ever, I failed." Chris replied, 'there's no fucking way.' It would be at least a week before I got my result. No time to retake it before

I ran out of money. If I failed, I would have to move back to Texas, back in with my ex.

~ No Calls. No Scores ~

I went ahead and started applying for jobs in Oklahoma. I started with Wal-Mart and Sam's, my last employer. I asked my current DM in Texas for a reference, and he quickly obliged. I did a phone interview thinking it was my way back but still terrified of being in a public facing position. I was afraid of being disabled from covid again, but then again, I had no choice. I also applied to a handful of other positions, one of which was completely out of my wheelhouse, a closed-door pharmacy. I would be safer there. I didn't receive a call back on anything that I threw out there. When I graduated from pharmacy college, I had ten offers before I even graduated. The climate was completely different now and I was feeling every bit of the temperature shift in the job market. I still had a job in DFW if I needed it, but I would have to move back in with my ex and the reduction in stress was finally allowing me to heal and get stronger. Something had to go my way, right?

Here's the thing. They no longer give scores on pharmacy exams. All you get to know is whether you pass or fail. So, if you fail, you don't even get to know if you were close. If you just needed to study harder or if you studied wrong all together. It was a long week, and I checked the site incessantly. I was driving home from Dallas and my phone dinged with an e-mail notification. It was from the Oklahoma State Board of Pharmacy. I passed! I was going to be able to stay in Oklahoma. I had to interview with the board, but that was mostly a formality. I was all but licensed. The tide was finally turning in my favor.

~ The Lesser of Evils ~

Much like when I got laid off in 2017, I did the unthinkable. I logged into CVS.com and searched for pharmacist positions. You see when you apply to CVS you have to take a psychological test of sorts to be considered for a position to ensure you are a proper fit. The way to beat this test is as follows, you simply select the answer that would correlate with making your work life the most miserable day in and day out. For example, it would ask, would you rather work in an environment that allows you plenty of time to complete daily tasks or option B provide excellent patient care while you are engulfed in flames? I exaggerate of course, but not by much. I worked for them before and knew what to expect. I told Chris and he shook his head no. I told him that I would keep looking, but they were always hiring. His reply? "For good reason brother, this scares me." I said, "me too, but I crumbled before because I had stress at work AND at home." He knew a little something about that himself, he gave me a reluctant nod and said, "I hope you are right." I told him that I quit without notice that last time that I worked for them and probably wouldn't even get a call back anyway and kept applying for jobs as the clock was continuing to tick down. I was licensed, yes, but I still needed the opportunity to use that license and start generating some income.

The very next day I got a request to interview with CVS. I was flabbergasted but scheduled the interview. I took my dress shirts and slacks to the dry cleaners, even though it was a virtual interview. I could have worn boxers, but was so desperate for a job, hell I even wore dress shoes. I got into full interview mode and attire. The interview was standard in nature and went as expected. I interview well, much thanks to the gift of gab that I inherited from my mother. I was a seasoned pharmacist now and even though they had kept building more and more pharmacy colleges until there was now a surplus of pulses to be pill dispensers, I still had a draw because I had over a decade of experience and a good track record with CVS, apart from the whole losing my shit and yanking my license off the wall thing. Then I got the question that I knew was coming.... Who was your district manager in east Texas? I gave her the name and quickly followed it with, he doesn't like me very much. She asked me, "why not?"

~ *You Don't Get Me Anymore* ~

Of course she would ask why not? I told her that I ripped my license down without notice. Her tone didn't change much, but instead I was asked why I would do such a thing. I explained that I took a vacation, a cruise to Cozumel. As I boarded the ship I received a call from my sister in Houston. My father had taken a turn for the worse and wasn't expected to make it through the night. I told her that we would turn around and drive to Houston. I didn't want to miss the final moments with my last parent. My sister stopped me from doing so, explaining that he wasn't "there" anymore. That he wouldn't know if I was there and to go on vacation and try to have fun with my family.

I reluctantly boarded the ship, and we set sail. One of the main reasons that I liked going on cruises is that my cell phone didn't have a signal. This made me unreachable by CVS. It was a true break from work. I could pretend that the professional side of me did not exist for 5 days. We got the 'all you can drink' package. For those not in the know, that is 16 drinks in a 24-hour period. My wife said, "there is no way you can drink that much in a day." Combine job stress, a failing marriage and my last parent dying while I was at sea. I said, "hold my beer or rather not."

I had a decent time, but as we set sail for home, I just knew the news that would be awaiting me when I returned to Galveston. My last parent would be gone. I would have once again missed the last breath of a parent. I once again got the urge to not be here anymore. I would go for walks on the cruise ship at night. I would look overboard at the dark swirls on the gulf abyss, and it was somehow welcoming. I would lean towards it physically and emotionally. Once again, I stayed for the kids. I concentrated on them and filled the days and nights with as much fun and memory making moments as I possibly could.

As we returned from international waters and got close to port, my phone went crazy. Some 200 plus text messages bombarded my phone all at once. Not even one was from my sister, instead they were all from work. A stark reminder of how much bullshit I had to put up with daily. None of those text messages were urgent, just typical corporate stuff, checklists and what not. The first person that I needed to check in with was my sister about arrangements for my father. I called my sister. My father was still alive! Not conscious but still breathing. I called my staff pharmacist to see if he'd cover me for a few days, he agreed. I then called my boss and said, "I need to go hold my father's hand." I was informed that I was out of PTO and that bereavement does not start until the family member passes away. My reply? "Tell me. Tell me that I cannot go hold my dying father's hand." He said, "you get one day." I took it and drove from Galveston to our home in east Texas. It was a race against time. A race that I had yet to win in terms of making it to a dying relative in time.

As I got home, I received a call back on a phone interview in DFW. They wanted an in-person interview and asked when I could make it. I said that I could make it that day at noon. It put me at risk of missing my father's last breath, but I needed a less stressful job for my health, and my father would have wanted it. I drove from east Texas to DFW, did the in-person interview and then drove south to Houston. He was still hanging on.

I walked into the room to see a hospice nurse and my sister. She looked exhausted and hugged me. Every death since my mother's passing reminded me of her. His breathing was agonal, they assured me that he couldn't feel it, but how could he not? He was still in there somewhere, right? I held his hand in mine, kissed his forehead and told him that he could let go. That I had made it. He died in 1998 when my mother passed, he just hadn't been buried yet. It was time.

Time was paradoxical that day. It simultaneously flew and crawled. I hated to leave, but had to go back to work as my job was being threatened. I drove home and went to work the next morning explaining to my staff that my father was still "alive", but I was forced to come back to work. They were furious. I was furious. My wife made plans to go have a game night with my daughter's friend's family, and I obliged reluctantly.

I sat down at the table and played cards and tried to relax. My phone rang and it was my brother-in-law. Hospice called him and let them know that my father had just drawn his last breath. He died alone. I was upset and relieved at the same time. I simply hoped that he had gotten to be reunited with mom, despite his actions after his mental state deteriorated. Not 15 minutes later my phone rang again. It was the DM for the job that I had interviewed with in DFW the day before. They offered me the job. I asked for 24 hours to give an answer. They obliged. My mind was still reeling from being an adult orphan, if there is such a thing. It was an odd feeling. Still processing all of it, my phone rang once again. This time it was my realtor; we got a good offer on the house. Dead father, job offer and sold a house within one hour. It was divinely chaotic, but a push toward making my decision on the employment front. What came next sealed the deal.

My phone dinged again, and I was informed that I had not reached my flu shot goal and that I would be setting up a table on my weekend off, without pay, on my days off until I had met their metric. I replied, "okay", but it wasn't. The next morning, which was supposed to be my day off, I walked in, pulled my license down and turned in my keys. The store manager said, "no, no, no. Don't leave like this man." I said, "I just watched my father die in pain. He worked his ass off his entire life and was treated like shit for it. You don't get me anymore."

Now the district manager that I was interviewing with in Oklahoma took in an abbreviated version of this story. She absorbed my reasoning on why my old distract manager probably didn't like me very much. She stated she didn't blame me one bit for yanking my license off the wall and asked when I could start. I told her the following week, but as I had my plans set, she would call me back with a change of heart a few days later.

~ Leaning In and Looking Forward ~

Upon closer inspection of my performance at my previous stores...she changed her mind. She had a new plan. I was offered my own store; more pay and a longer commute. It was more stressful in every way imaginable, but my ego said go for it. It would allow me to financially dig out faster and eventually fight for custody of my son. I took it on. I leaned into it, gritting my teeth, I leaned into it.

It was an hour commute each way, and it was a busy store. Come to find out, the store had been routinely going through about three pharmacy managers a year for the past few years.

It was not what I wanted to hear, but I was driven to succeed and money motivated. The key to longevity was going to be balance. I had mastered the art of mental and physical recovery over the past 4 months, but there was a catch. I was on disability. I did not have work bearing down on me. Time management would be the biggest issue.

~ *Let's Go for a Ride Brother* ~

I had my first weekend off and Chris snagged me in the kitchen. He said, "You got plans today brother." It wasn't a question; it was a statement. I said, "oh yeah?" He said, "Let's go for a ride brother." I hopped in his car riding shotgun, and he grinned and said, "today is the day. Your daughter has a point, and you made a promise." I knew exactly what he meant. He said, "today, you are getting your first tattoo." He put $500 in my hand, and we drove down to 23rd street in OKC. He made an appointment, and I met with my tattoo artist to finalize the vision. I had never stood in a tattoo parlor before, but I was somehow at ease. I told him my vision and the placement. He looked at me and confirmed that this was indeed my first tattoo. He said, "bro that is a good amount of real estate for your first tat."

I lay on the table and he asked about my pain tolerance as it would be about a two-hour process. I told him that I was a bit of an anomaly and that some things that are supposed to hurt didn't, while others that shouldn't be that bad can be agonizing. I reiterated that I would get through no matter what the scenario. Once he got me talking about my story, he understood the meaning and passion behind it. As I recounted the events that led me to be in the tattoo parlor that day, he just shook his head. He said, "brother you are a walking, talking miracle" and that I should write a book. I told him that the process was already underway. He wanted me to let him know when the book came out and I grinned and agreed. I left with a sore arm and a renewed spirit to stay, Unkillable for as long as possible. Ben, if you are reading this, I still love the tat brother!

~ Running Low on Time ~

I fell back into the routine that I had adopted in my more stressful days from 2012 through 2014. Running in the darkness so I wouldn't lose time with Stoney 2.0 to the fitness part of my healing journey. Since I was devoting so much time to commuting and working. It left him to his own devices for a good majority of the day, but he was still happy to be in control of his environment and to be drama free. So, my days started around 4am to keep cardio and my weight training on track so I didn't lose any of the precious ground that I had gained in the past few months. It was exhausting, but it was my first taste of independence that I had in quite some time, even though I was still living with my best friend, even though I was declaring bankruptcy, and I had no idea what I was going to do when they repossessed my car. Those were tomorrow's problems, and I was fighting through enough just to get through the days as they were.

~ Spotting....A Problem ~

I was back in the flow, if that is even possible in retail pharmacy. Truth be told, I was drowning. The commute was hard on me, but the job itself wore on me faster than anticipated. I kept to my routine, but the added stress of the pharmacist in charge position almost immediately wore me out at a faster rate than I could fight it with meds and selfcare. I tried to pretend that I was alright, but I wasn't. It took its toll on me mentally as well. My staff was strong, but it didn't matter. The industry had changed. The pharmacists, which had been in such high demand just a few years ago, were now so expendable. They just kept building pharmacy colleges. When I got into the pharmacy program in 2006, one applicant got accepted for every 11 that applied. Now the latest number that I saw for my alma mater was one for every 1.6. It was insane, it is not what was sold to me as a profession. Instead of being able to stand your ground and demand more help, you now just accepted the working conditions, because there were dozens of pharmacists just wanting a position. We went from a shortage to an absolute glut of pharmacists. Much like my profession, I could feel my health unraveling again.

My district manager knew that the load of that store was wearing on me. She showed up out of nowhere and saw the chaos but also saw me trying my level best. She pulled me aside and explained that she could see me quitting and she didn't want that, not at all. As with most open management positions, there is usually a good reason for the opening. She had served me a shit burger, she knew it, and I had taken the biggest bite of my career.

I walked in one morning and I could feel it. I couldn't see it yet, but I could feel it. I was shaking and my tech could see it. She asked if I was okay, I replied yes, but check this out. I pointed to multiple joints on my hands. She asked what she was supposed to see. I said, "nothing yet, but I'll show you again at the end of the shift." We were both working bell to bell that day. She looked confused and concerned. I told her that she would understand when we closed later that day. She couldn't believe what she would see later that day.

I told her that morning that I could feel it coming on. In pharmacy college I learned something that I never thought that I would relate to so frequently, but here I was. The lesson? That blood, blood ANYWHERE, outside of a vessel or artery is an irritant. That morning, I felt the familiar irritation, the burning, the acidic foreshadowing of a dermatomyositis flare. It was unmistakable. As I closed the gate on the pharmacy that day, worn, beaten and exhausted, I called my tech over once more and showed her my hands.

Her eyes grew wide, as if she was watching all the small scenes of an M. Night Shyamalan movie being woven together. I had blood blisters on the exact locations that I had pointed to that very morning. She teared up and asked what it meant. I explained that I wasn't strong enough to keep doing what I was doing at that store. That in effect it was stealing away every inch of recovery that I had fought so very hard to gain over the last six months. She could tell that I had to leave, but I had nowhere to go. My district manager showed up again the next day.

She had a plan to keep me aboard CVS. She knew what I was up against, both in terms of health and the store that I had taken on. She could see the times that I would turn the alarm on and off for the pharmacy. I was going in an hour and a half early and staying 2 hours after close and still lost ground because of staffing. It is hard, to right a ship that is already sinking. She moved me to a store closer to home, not by a lot, but it trimmed 20 minutes off my commute each direction. I was still exhausted, but it was somewhat better. Despite her efforts to prevent what she saw months earlier; it was too late. I settled in as best I could but kept getting worse and worse. I felt disabled again. I was desperate again. I needed a way out. It was damned if I do and damned if I don't. No matter the choice that I made, I would likely falter either way. Then I found something that just might work, it was a risk, but I took it.

~ I Need a Consult ~

In the world of ever receding profit margins in the world of pharmacy, a new 'task' was born, medication therapy management. I was good at it; in effect it was counseling the patient. As Doc Holiday would say, don't make no mistake, at the retail level it was about money. I had heard grumblings years earlier that Medicare was going to rate pharmacies using a star system based on patient outcomes. In essence, making sure that patients didn't miss doses and that their therapies were safe, but at the same time cost efficient. Whether that meant the cost of the medication itself, or the evidence of reduced hospitalizations of patients with certain health conditions. As my pharmacy business professor so profoundly put it, if there is ever ANYTHING that you don't understand, anything at all, not just in the world of pharmacy. All you must do is follow the money and you will find your answer.

In retail, it was a task on top of everything else, but with this job it was the ONLY task. That made it easier from a mental aspect. On top of that, it was work from home. It was safer for me. It would be less exposure to infectious disease, whether it be COVID, the flu, patients coming in with staph infections, whatever it may be that could trigger a flare. I was safer. However, there was one aspect that was a risk, and I didn't have the resources that I needed. Once again, enter my best friend.

Their software made having an iPhone and an iPad necessary. I had neither, nor did I have the money to secure them. Chris was happy that my days of commuting would come to an end. There was no I told you so, but rather once again, I've got you. He walked in and handed me an iPhone and an iPad. Now it was up to me to make this thing work, however there was still a challenge.

The challenge was that I was cold calling patients. It wasn't like in retail, where my patients knew me, I was an unknown. Just some dude calling to talk about their health and medications, their personal stuff. In a world where senior citizens are primary targets for the nefarious walkers of planet earth, I had to find a way to gain their trust enough for them to confide in me about their health.

I have a knack for getting people to open up, but this was the next level. It was commission based, but with a base salary, or so I thought. The fine print got me. I was so desperate to get out of CVS, I jumped into the murky waters of commission-based income. I had a safety net, my rent was paid, but I still had an insane amount in child support garnished, even though my son was with me, and then there was the alimony. I enjoyed the position, and I was getting stronger again, but it wasn't long before I realized that I wasn't even treading water, I was drowning, not health wise, but monetarily.

I once again logged into Indeed.com and threw my line into the overpopulated waters of pharmacists. I was once again on the hunt for a more palatable flavor of occupational dissatisfaction. Nothing. Nothing. Nothing. I was sinking. I was angry. So, I did what I did in my twenties when life's stresses were getting the best of me.

~ Practicing and Changing Practices ~

In my younger days, I would decompress by throwing the ball. My first 'love' was bowling. I would practice. Practice, that word would mean vastly different things as my life progressed. It went from preparing for tournaments in my teens and twenties to how I would provide care to my patients in my thirties and forties.

Like my love life, bowling always seemed to be fickle. I didn't always get out of it what I put into it and at times I got in my own way like no one else could dream of, but I loved it and that would never change. I wasn't what I used to be, but it always seemed to help. I always seemed to be in a better headspace when I finished a practice session. The world melted away, if just for a bit. Did it solve my problem.... no....but there was a connection to the solution. In my mind, it was a sign.

I lugged my stuff back to my car. I sat in the driver's seat, sweaty and still having no real solution, but somehow less stressed. I replaced some cortisol with some dopamine and my mind was quieter than it was when I walked into the bowling center. I started my drive home and my phone rang. It was not likely that it was a bill collector as I had already gone bankrupt, so there was less dread when answering an unknown number than there had been in quite some time. I answered with an overly unprofessional, YELLOW!

A man's voice said, "This is Roger the pharmacist in charge, I looked at your resume and was wondering if you were still looking for a job as a staff pharmacist?" I was shocked, as I had gotten used to the canned speech in email format of thank you for your application, but at this time we are pursuing other candidates, but we will keep your resume on file.

I replied, "yessir", as I was drenched in sweat on a sweltering July afternoon in Oklahoma. He said, "I hate to ask, but are you available to come in NOW for an interview?" I panicked. I explained that I had just gone bowling and was wearing a backwards hat, a sweaty t-shirt and cargo shorts. He said he didn't care. I replied that I cared and wanted to show respect for him and his pharmacy. I told him that I could be there in an hour and a half. He obliged.

I took the world's fastest shower and looked at my file on Indeed. I had applied to this position months ago. A position that I thought, in all honesty, I had no chance of getting. It was a completely different practice setting. It was a closed-door setup, the door that was cracked open for me was closed door.

I liked the idea of being nonpatient facing. It took away a great deal of the risk of catching a virus or other infection that could trigger a flare or yet another autoimmune disease. This is what I needed, so much so, that I was nervous. I never got nervous in interviews, once I got to that point, if I got into a room, I felt like the position was mine. This time, however, it was different.

I drove across OKC not really knowing what to expect. I pulled up to the location, a large building that resembled a warehouse. I rang the bell and was welcomed in by a young lady that said, "Roger will be right with you." I was in the room with another gentleman, who was holding a portfolio. I hadn't shared space with my competition since my pharmacy college interview. It was surreal. We exchanged pleasantries, none of which I can specifically recall. Before I knew it, an older man called the other gentleman in, and the door closed only to reopen quickly. He poked his head back out of the door and said, "don't be discouraged, I am looking for two pharmacists."

The other gentleman's interview was quick, even with my fate hanging in the balance and me imagining all the worst-case scenarios. My fellow applicant made his way past me and Roger called my name. I had no idea what I was walking in to, but was excited to do so, not only because it was different, but because I knew the stresses of my old practice setting would surely do me in within months.

~ *The Tours* ~

The tours started. You read that right, not a tour, but tours. We made our way through the building. The various facets of the operation. The pharmacists did not have a look of dread on their faces. They had time to converse with me and we started joking a bit while we recounted some of our horror stories of our time in retail pharmacies. I remember Roger looking at me and saying, "I can tell that you are a smart guy, I believe you can do this. It will be different than anything you've done, but I think you are more than capable young man." He then asked if I had time to do a conference call with the district manager as he wanted her input on me as well. I agreed and that was when the 'tour' of ME started.

We proceeded to his office, and we sat across the desk from each other. He dialed the phone as I sat and realized that I had not handled the interview as I had so many in the past. I hadn't brought up my health struggles, I was just me and that got me a seat at the desk. That got me to the person of influence, the person that I knew would ultimately either give Roger the greenlight to hire me or not. She answered and said good afternoon. Roger said, "I've got Stoney here and I think he could be a good fit, but I would like you to talk with him."

The obligatory pleasantries gave way to the tougher question. "What sets you apart from all the other applicants Stoney?" I told her that I would answer honestly even though it could hurt my chances of acquiring the position. I told her that my greatest strength is also my greatest weakness. She inquisitively asked how so. I explained my history of Guillain Barre in pharmacy school, the host of other health issues and the turn my personal life had taken as a result. I explained that I was once in a skilled nursing unit that they currently had under contract to supply their medications. I explained that I knew what it was like to feel helpless, to wake up one morning on zero medications and the next day be on twenty. I went on to convey that this allows me to surpass the regular empathy of most healthcare professionals, because I have been there and still am there to some extent. I explained that my strength is that of compassion through coexistence with those who are chronically ill and as such it makes me a better healthcare provider, albeit physically weaker. I explained that I would have doctor appointments and there could come a time that I spent a few days in the hospital if things go awry again, but I am good at what I do and that the ability to serve patients who are in the position that I used to live in would give my occupation more meaning than it had ever had before.

Roger sat in silence across the desk. His eyes welled with tears as he listened to the road that had led me to this desk that day. He was in shock that this strong looking applicant was carrying so much pain and struggle on his shoulders and in his heart for the past 14 years. I could hear her voice shake; I heard her sniffle and clear her throat on the other end of the line. We ended the call, and he walked me out. I would receive a call the next morning with an offer for the position. It was what I needed, it was what I wanted and what was meant to be all along. As time passed after I had worked there for months and years, I would thank him for the opportunity that he gave me. He shrugged it off at first, but we got to know each other better and better. He would pick up on my rougher days and ask if I was okay on a regular basis. He had faced his own struggles, and our paths were similar in some ways. I told him that I believed that he saved my life by getting me out of retail. He told me that when he heard me tell my story on that conference call that he saw something in me. I asked what he saw. He said, "I saw a man that needed to catch a break, and I was honored to be able to give him a chance."

~ Tik-Tok My Friend ~

I have been an over sharer ever since I came out of my shell in my teens. This got kicked into overdrive when I got Guilain Barre. Those runs in the darkness between 2012 and 2014 introduced me to the world of motivational speakers. I filled my mind with the likes of Les Brown, Tony Robbins, Eric Thomas, Zig Ziglar and countless others while my legs carried me up and down those winding country roads in East Texas. I began posting inspirational quotes on Facebook along with my mileages for the day. I soon replaced other's words with my own and just kept showing up for myself. Posting on social media was a secondary form of accountability for me. I didn't have thousands of friends on Facebook, just 200 or so, but each of them knew the struggles that I had faced over the years. That was a catalyst for the nudges.

I had been urged for a while to start a Tik-Tok, they said that the world needed some hope and some positivity and that my story and mindset could provide just that. I knew NOTHING about running any sort of social media. I downloaded the app during the pandemic, like most of us did, but it never crossed my mind to be a creator. I struggled with my username, but then I remembered what my daughter said during my cancer scare during my dermatomyositis diagnosis. That day she looked at her father shaking and bleeding from dermatomyositis not knowing what the future was going to hold. Our eyes met and I told her that daddy would beat it like he had beaten everything else. She said, "of course you will dad, you're unkillable." Unkillable Positivity was born.

I had the account but held my phone in my hands for weeks. I couldn't conjure any creative juices; the words just wouldn't flow. Then I had an especially rough night. I had fought for so long, so hard, then I felt like I was once again slipping backwards. I awoke in so much pain that morning that it took me an hour just to get out of bed. I limped to the bathroom and took off my clothes. Then I saw it.

I was failing, yet another therapy. My dermatomyositis was causing me to bleed through my clothes again. I lathered myself in steroid cream and got into the car to head to the gym. My arms and legs were weak. I looked into the rearview mirror and got my inspiration. I could hear my best friend's voice echo in my head. "just start talking bro." I pressed record and did just that. It was rough, unpolished, and nothing like I had seen anyone else do on TikTok. I hit record with sunken, fatigued eyes and my backwards Cleveland Indian's hat, it went as follows:

"You know, I had trouble getting up today. I fight health struggles every day. This morning, I had trouble getting up to fight. I asked myself what I keep doing it all for? I couldn't come up with a sustainable answer. I had nothing. I asked myself a different question. I asked myself who I was doing it all for? My kids spring to mind. They are the second part to that answer. The first part has to be me. Because if you can't endure your trials for you, then you can't be there to help anyone else when their trials come along. To help the ones that you love endure. So, endure for you, that way you can be there to help others endure their struggles. Have a good day."

I hit post. I didn't know how to edit. I didn't know how to do anything but place a hashtag or two and hope for the best. As of the writing of this paragraph, TikTok has yet to be banned, but there is another bill being passed that puts it in danger. If it is still there as you read this, my first TikTok is still up, raw and unedited. TikTok and social media have enriched my life in more ways than I ever imagined that it could. If you have followed me for quite some time, you know that there are certainly more stories to tell, but that is for a later time. If I have learned anything from this experience it is that you don't have to start your journey perfectly, but much rather, you just need to start. You make your strides. You make your mistakes, but more than that, you somehow make your way. In your darkest times, you move toward the light and in those times that there is no light to be seen, you move as if you can, because the light is there, whether you can see it or not. You may not be as efficient as you had hoped to be and you will likely experience more detours and delays than you can imagine but just keep moving. Much like this book, and myself for that matter, it was far from perfect, but it is something that I felt in my soul, was the path that I was destined to follow. So, I followed the light, no matter how dim it seemed. If you have followed me on social media, I will end this message as I always do. Until next time, Y'all be a force for good.

Printed in Dunstable, United Kingdom